THE ULTIMATE
Air Fryer
COOKBOOK

To my mum, the most incredible woman I know.
Without you none of this would have happened.
Thank you – I love you.

PENGUIN MICHAEL JOSEPH

UK | USA | Canada | Ireland | Australia
India | New Zealand | South Africa

Penguin Michael Joseph is part of the Penguin Random House group of companies
whose addresses can be found at global.penguinrandomhouse.com

Penguin
Random House
UK

First published 2023
009

Set in Tellumo
Design by Georgie Hewitt
Food styling by Katy McClelland and Troy Willis
Colour reproduction by Altaimage Ltd
Printed and bound in Italy by L.E.G.O. S.p.A.

The authorized representative in the EEA is Penguin Random House Ireland,
Morrison Chambers, 32 Nassau Street, Dublin D02 YH68

A CIP catalogue record for this book is available from the British Library

ISBN: 978–0–241–63757–9

www.greenpenguin.co.uk

MIX
Paper | Supporting
responsible forestry
FSC® C018179

Penguin Random House is committed to a
sustainable future for our business, our readers
and our planet. This book is made from Forest
Stewardship Council® certified paper.

THE ULTIMATE
Air Fryer
COOKBOOK

Quick, healthy, energy-saving recipes for every occasion

Clare Andrews

MICHAEL JOSEPH

Contents

Introd

uction

Welcome

Thank you so much for buying this book and coming with me on this journey. Perhaps you've had an air fryer for a while and are looking for some new ideas, perhaps you've just bought your first one and don't know where to start – either way, I'm very pleased to have you here. I think it's likely that many of you will be buying this as a response to the cost-of-living crisis and are trying to find a more economical alternative to the oven. The good news is that you're in the right place. The even better news is that air fryers are not just a low-energy alternative to the traditional oven or fryer, they are also quicker and healthier. Win, win, win!

My own air-fryer journey began back at the start of the COVID-19 lockdowns. I've always had a passion for cooking and a love of food, but when my lovely mum bought me an air fryer as a gift I can honestly say that I had no idea what to cook in it! I did some research online and everything just seemed so incredibly beige – I like chips as much as the next person, but I was sure that there must be a way of using the air fryer to make the kind of vibrant, healthy meals that I liked to cook regularly in my oven. So, I took myself on a journey and decided to document it on my Instagram account (@airfryeruk) so that I had a record of what worked and what didn't, how long certain foods took to cook, what ingredients worked well, and so on. Before long, other people started to follow the account and like my posts, and the page has continued to grow and grow from that point. I know that social media has a dark side, but building such a fantastic community, all of whom are supportive and inquisitive, has been a really positive experience for me. It's so wonderful to know there will always be someone to ask for advice or reach out to – air-fryer related or not! For me, it's been such an amazing ride and long may it continue.

Once I started to use my air fryer more, I quickly noticed that my energy bill was creeping down and, in recent months (I'm writing this in November 2022, when energy costs are spiralling), it has been a real life-saver. I do, of course, still use my oven, but now I tend to save it only for batch cooking, rather than putting it on for a single jacket potato or the odd chicken breast. If I'm roasting a chicken for a crowd, for example, I'll also throw in some jacket potatoes for the week ahead and maybe cook a curry or Bolognese on the hob at the same so that I can freeze them for future meals. If I'm cooking a single meal for myself and my family, it's being cooked in the air fryer. (Even that same roast chicken will go in the air fryer as long as I'm not feeding a huge crowd and need a really big bird.) Once I started seeing the benefits to my energy bills, I also started being more mindful of other ways of saving money and reducing food waste. I'll never shop for fresh veg if I've got stuff already that needs using up in the fridge – even if I don't have quite what I need for a recipe then I'll adapt and work with what I already have. I'd advise you to do the same – you might even end up with something you like better! I find cooking this way really rewarding (literally, when it comes to saving money!). We should all be trying to reduce food waste as much as possible. It's better for your wallet and, crucially, it's far better for the planet, so always try and have a trawl for those fridge-raid meals before succumbing to the call of the supermarket!

What's grown from me experimenting by throwing a few ingredients together and cooking them in the air fryer to share with my son (by far my most honest critic!) round our kitchen table, has turned into the most amazing adventure that has culminated in being asked to write this book! I so hope what's contained in these pages will help and inspire you in some way, even if just a couple of the recipes make it into your weekly favourites. The recipes are just guidelines, so as you get more confident with the air fryer then feel free to mix it up. Want more chilli? Throw it in! Don't like the flavour of cumin? Bung in some ground coriander instead! My only advice would be to learn the basics before trying to break the rules.

I hope you enjoy this book as much as I've enjoyed creating these recipes for you.

Clare

What is an Air Fryer?

On their most basic level air fryers are more convenient, compact, quicker and cheaper-to-run alternatives to traditional ovens. The word 'fryer' in the name can trip people up a bit, but really they're mini convection ovens that need minimal (if any) preheating and are much smaller, so you're not paying (or waiting) for a cavernous space to heat up to cook your food in. Anything that you would cook in the oven or under the grill can be cooked in an air fryer – as long as it fits! And that's not the end of it, you can also bake cakes and pastry and even boil and poach eggs!

Air fryers work by circulating hot air rapidly around the food in the basket. The powerful fan whooshes all of that heat (and the tiny bit of oil that you may have added) around the food, allowing it to crisp-up wonderfully with very little fat. It's perfectly possible to use the air fryer without oil, too, in which case the results are more like a conventional oven. Many newer air fryers have multiple settings, for things like roasting, baking and dehydrating, which do things like automatically reducing the temperature and fan speed to suit that type of cooking.

There are so many different varieties of air fryer on the market now – it's hard to keep up. If you're new to air frying, I'd suggest cooking a few freezer basics (fish fingers, chips, etc) before diving in and trying to roast a whole joint of meat! Some air fryers will run hotter than others, some will be larger, some varieties have multiple drawers so that you can cook more than thing at a time. Take some time to get to know your own air fryer before trying to cook anything too elaborate. I want you to feel confident – it's like anything new, daunting at first, but cook a few dishes and I'm sure you'll fall in love with using it as much as I did. The most important advice I can give you is to experiment and mix it up! Air fryers aren't just for chips (though they do make really good ones!). I've had countless conversations with people who have bought an air fryer, made chips or wedges a couple of times and then banished the machine to the back of the cupboard, which is such a shame! Forget the word 'fryer' and re-frame your air fryer as an air 'oven' and that might help you see its limitless possibilities!

Do Your Homework

Before you cook anything in your air fryer, always read the manufacturers' instructions. I've tried to keep the recipe instructions very general in this book, but depending on the brand and model, there might be different requirements around preheating your air fryer or not before you add your food. (I like to preheat for a couple of minutes because I find the food cooks more evenly.) But what works for one air fryer may not another, so get to know yours! You may cook a few recipes that don't turn out as planned at first – that's OK! Learn from what mistakes were made and you'll know for next time.

The Benefits of Air Frying

For many people, myself included, this is where the air-frying journey starts. Why air fry? What are the benefits? Is there more to air frying than the sea of beige food that is associated with deep-fat frying? The answer is, '100% yes!'. They are also up to 80% cheaper to run than your standard convection oven, much faster and can be a lot healthier too! In this section we can explore these benefits.

Air Fryers are Cheaper

Air fryers are significantly cheaper to run than a traditional oven, and with the current economic conditions, these wonderful machines can really help keep your costs down. Why heat up an entire oven for a single portion? There's just no need. By using your air fryer regularly, you really will see a tangible saving on your energy bills. They consume significantly less energy than a conventional oven, which also makes cooking your food faster and more effective. So, yes, overall, an air fryer will save you money, but it's important to purchase a machine that's suitable for your family's needs. If you have a large family, you need a large air fryer. You don't want to be have to cook multiple batches or to also put the oven on to cook your meals! Always do your research and read the reviews.

Air Fryers are Quicker

Because the space inside of an air-fryer basket is far smaller than an oven, it heats up much more quickly and the high-powered fan circulates the hot air around your food at a much faster rate, meaning that meals cook in less time than they might in your oven. All of the recipes in this book include cooking times, but I also want you to be able to use your air fryer for basics – we've all reached for the frozen waffles and fish fingers when the kids are hangry after a long day! With things like this, follow the packet instructions and you may end up with burnt food. Use the charts overleaf to make adjustments for cooking these kind of foods in your air fryer.

Cooking Time & Temperature Conversion Charts

TIME IN OVEN	TIME IN AIR FRYER
	8 mins
10 mins	12 mins
15 mins	16 mins
20 mins	20 mins
25 mins	25 mins
30 mins	28 mins
35 mins	32 mins
40 mins	35 mins
45 mins	40 mins
50 mins	45 mins
55 mins	48 mins
1 hour	

OVEN TEMP	FAN OVEN TEMP	AIR FRYER TEMP
	170°C	150°C
190°C	180°C	160°C
200°C	190°C	170°C
210°C	200°C	180°C
220°C	210°C	190°C
230°C		

Air Fryers are Healthier

One of the health benefits when using an air fryer is that you generally don't need to add any oil, though for dishes that you might traditionally cook in a deep-fat fryer or roast in lots of oil, you can get wonderfully crisp results by using just a teaspoon or so. This means you can still enjoy those wonderfully crunchy roasties or crispy chips but with far less fat involved in the cooking. If you do decide to use oil, always add it straight onto your food and give everything a toss to coat, rather than adding to your basket – this will mean everything cooks uniformly and also helps when it comes to clean your air fryer (more on that later). As to what type of oil to use, I suggest vegetable oil, avocado oil or olive oil. You can purchase a variety of spray oils too, including low-calorie cooking sprays. Read your manufacturer's instructions for guidance on these, because some recommend not using them in case they damage the machine. You can buy nifty little spray bottles to add your own olive (or other) oils to for the same effect, so if you're air-frying regularly one of those is a worthwhile investment. If you are cooking frozen food, like chips, you don't need to add any oil – it's simply not necessary.

Beyond the beige, air fryers are wonderful at cooking veg quickly. I use mine for everything from wonderfully crispy kale and roasted broccoli, to roasted parsnips, stuffed tomatoes and even softening veg quickly to blend into soup.

Which Air Fryer Should I Buy?

This is the number one question that I get asked by my family, friends and followers. Air fryers come in shapes and sizes to suit all different households and budgets, so it really is down to your individual needs. If you've got the money to spend, it is easy to be seduced by one of the huge, all-singing, all-dancing premium varieties, but bear in mind that this doesn't make sense if you're mostly cooking for just one or two people as, in terms of energy saving, smaller is better. These fryers also take up a lot of counter space, so have a look at the dimensions and work out if you have space in your kitchen before committing to purchase. Ideally you want a 10-cm gap all the way around your air fryer whilst it is in use to keep your appliance from overheating. Mine gets used so regularly that it lives on the kitchen counter all of the time, but you may want to keep yours in a cupboard or hidden out of the way on a shelf, so do bear in mind that they can be hefty!

In terms of the types of air fryers available, the two main types are the larger air-fryer ovens and the smaller basket fryers, often called tower air fryers. Both essentially do the same thing, though the tower fryers take up less space and generally have a smaller capacity. The air-fryer ovens often have multiple drawers, meaning that you can cook different components of a meal at different temperatures at the same time, which makes them ideal for larger families or preparing more complex recipes that have multiple elements. You can also get rotisserie air fryers that contain a rotating spit and are designed specifically for cooking big pieces of meat. These look great, but I'd only recommend them if you're going to be doing this kind of cooking very regularly.

If you are someone who wants to use your air fryer for cooking larger pieces of meat, such as a whole chicken or a joint of beef or pork, then you'll need a large air fryer that has the necessary capacity. These larger air fryers can cost well over £200, so make sure that you really are going to use it regularly before investing. If you have a friend who is always telling you how brilliant their air fryer is (I am that friend to my own friends!), maybe ask them if you can have a play with theirs before committing to your own purchase.

Does the air fryer you're looking to purchase have a pull-out tray or basket? These are great as they allow you to easily check the progress of your food throughout the cooking time. Others come with a bowl and often have a viewing window in the lid so you can check the food without opening the basket section. It's all personal preference, but I prefer to be able to be able to pull my basket out and give it a quick shake halfway through cooking – this is especially useful for cooking foods like chips or wedges, as a quick shake redistributes the food in the basket and helps everything crisp up evenly. Some air fryers come with a paddle attachment that will turn the food for you as you cook, which can be useful when you're looking to get the food crispy on all sides (though shaking the basket every 5 minutes or so will do the same thing).

Other factors to consider are whether the air-fryer baskets can go in the dishwasher (this really varies between models, so is worth checking), what type of timer it has (an electronic digital timer is the most accurate), what pre-sets it comes with (more expensive air fryers will often have special settings for baking, roasting, crisping, etc) and customer reviews. The good news about air fryers being the new must-have item in the kitchen is that it's easy to find out what other people think of each model, so do your research!

Air fryer picked? You're good to go! This wonderful new appliance will enhance all your mealtimes from now on, whilst also keeping the costs down too.

Air-fryer Kit

Now that you've bought your air fryer and are ready to start cooking, is there anything else you need to get started? Though you can be up and running straight away, if you're going to be using your machine regularly (and why wouldn't you be?), there are a few bits of kit that it would be a good idea to invest in to make your air frying journey just that bit smoother. You don't have to buy all of this at once – build up your collection of kit over time as you work out the types of food that you like to cook in your air fryer. The list below is the kit that I use regularly. Do bear in mind that you need to make sure that anything you buy needs to fit inside your fryer – they come in all shapes and sizes, so do make a note of the dimensions of yours before going on a shopping spree!

Silicone Moulds

Silicone works really well in the air fryer because it is heatproof, comes in all shapes and sizes and washes up really easily. I use silicone cupcake cases for everything from baking cakes to poaching eggs. You can pick up a stack relatively cheaply from somewhere like Amazon or a dedicated cookware shop and they can be used over and over again, making them environmentally friendly as well as handy and economical.

Larger silicone moulds come in rectangular or circular shapes, so choose the one that best fits your air fryer. These are perfect for anything with a sauce that you might not want to put straight in the base of your air fryer. I use them for anything from stews and casseroles to roasting vegetables for soups. You can also use them for baking larger cakes as long as you grease them first.

Heatproof Ceramic Ramekins and Dishes

If you don't want to buy silicone moulds, heatproof ramekins and larger ceramic dishes make a great alternative. I like to use ramekins for things like my crustless quiches (page 67), where you're looking for an individual portion that will fill you up rather than something bite-sized. The bonus with these is that you've probably already got a few hiding at the back of your cupboard, so they're a great option for when you're first getting started. It's really important to make sure that the variety that you're using is fully heatproof as the last thing you want is shards of ceramic in your lovingly prepared food!

Oil Spray Bottle

If you want lovely crisp food in the air fryer, the good news is that you only need a fraction of the oil that you would use if you were shallow- or deep-frying the same food. A teaspoon or so is more than enough. You can toss the food in a little oil before adding to the fryer, but I like to use one of thr simple spray bottles that can be pumped up and then mists oil lightly over the food. I generally use olive oil in mine, though it would work just as well with other oils. Some people use low-calorie sprays in their air fryer, though I would caution against this. These sprays tend to have a lower burning point than traditional cooking oils and can damage the non-stick coating on the inside of your air fryer as a result. Using a fine mist of olive oil will add minimal calories and you'll still get lovely crisp food.

Meat Thermometer

For me, this is a must have. One of the brilliant things about cooking things in an air fryer is that food cooks quicker. The one downside of this is that cooking times on packets or in traditional recipes are often longer than needed, so you may need to do a bit of sleuthing to find out when certain foods are cooked through. A instant read thermometer gives an immediate temperature so that you know with confidence that your food is safe to eat. Though they are slightly more expensive, I prefer varieties with a digital display, as there is less room for error. Use the tables on pages 28–33 to work out the right temperature to cook your food to.

Air Fryer Racks

These tiered metal racks aren't essential by any means but they are nice to have, especially if you're going to be cooking for a crowd. By adding extra layers to your air-fryer drawer they are essentially doubling or tripling the surface area that you to have to cook on. These are great for things like fish fingers or chicken goujons, where you have lots of hungry mouths to feed and don't want to spend the time (or extra energy!) cooking multiple batches. A warning though, these are made of metal and do get very hot in the air fryer so it's important to be very careful when removing them as they can burn easily. I also find that the food on the top tier of the fryer (closest to the fan) cooks quicker than the food near the base, so you may want to swap the tiers around halfway through cooking time for even cooking.

Baking Paper

This is something that you will likely already have in your kitchen, but it's really useful and something that people might not immediately think is safe for the air fryer. Much like using it in the oven, baking paper won't burn in the air fryer, though it does need to be weighed down with food so that it doesn't blow around and touch the heating element when the fryer is closed. Use it to line the base of the the air-fryer drawer on foods that might otherwise be tricky to lift out, such as free-form pastry tarts, breaded chicken or fish, etc.

Air-Fryer Basics

The tips below act as a quick-start guide to using your air fryer and cover the kind of basic questions that I wish I had had the answers to when I started out on my own air-fryer journey.

Preheating

One of the best things about the air fryer is how quickly it comes up to temperature. Because the chamber is so much smaller than that of a conventional oven, it heats up much more quickly and, as a result, doesn't need to be preheated in the same way you would an oven. I know lots of people don't preheat their air fryers at all, but I find that a couple of minutes brings the air fryer up to temperature and results in more even cooking.

Cooking Frozen Foods

I use my air fryer every day in some way or another, though I don't always cook from scratch, as, let's face it, there's not always time! This is when your freezer can come in handy – fish fingers, scampi and, of course, the faithful frozen chip can all be cooked in your air fryer and, even better, won't take as much time as they would in the oven. The key to cooking frozen food in the air fryer and getting a lovely crisp finish is not to overfill. While it can be tempting to put as much food as you can fit in your drawer, this can prevent food from cooking evenly and mean that you get a lovely crisp top layer but the food at the bottom of the basket is soggy and unappealing. For things like frozen chips, my tip is to half-fill the drawer and shake the basket every five minutes or so to ensure that the heat is evenly distributed throughout the food while it is cooking.

You'll find a chart giving you some rough timings and temperatures for air-fried versus oven-cooked food on page 15, though it's always a good idea to check that the food is piping hot all the way through before serving, especially for anything involving meat or fish.

How Full Is Too Full?

Overfilling is the easiest thing to do when using your air fryer. While it's often tempting to add as much as you can, this will increase your cooking time and mean that your food may not cook evenly.

For most air-fryer cooking, it's best to spread the food out in a single layer at the base of the fryer basket or drawer and turn once or twice during cooking so that the food get crisp on all sides. Some fryers have crisper plates in the base which allow the hot air to bounce back up and crisp the food underneath as well as on top, so you may find that you don't not have to turn your food if your air fryer has this feature.

Reheating Foods

The air fryer is brilliant for breathing fresh life into day-old food. For anything that was crisp and delicious a day ago but is sad and soggy now, a few minutes in the air fryer will bring it straight back to life. This works especially well for things like pizza, nuggets or even day-old fries (it's also brilliant for adding that just-cooked crispness to takeaway chips). This doesn't work with all foods and it's best to stick to reheating in a pan or the microwave for anything saucy, like a curry or a casserole.

Cleaning

There is no single rule for how to clean an air fryer so you should always read the manufacturers' instructions for your particular model. Some air-fryer drawers will happily go in the dishwasher, others won't, which can be a factor to consider when choosing which air fryer you want to buy. That said, I rarely put my air-fryer drawer in the dish washer and find that it cleans up really easily with a bit of soapy water. Using baking paper in the base of your fryer will help avoid any really stubborn messes adhering to your basket.

Cooking Charts

Use the charts on the next few pages to work out how long you need to cook certain ingredients for. These timings are estimates and air fryers do differ, so make sure to always check that your food is cooked properly and to the correct temperature before consuming.

Chicken

INGREDIENT	AIR FRYER TEMP	TIME	INTERNAL FOOD TEMP	NOTES
Whole bird (approx. 1.6kg)	180°C	1 hour	75°C	Start breast-side down, turn after 30 mins
Breasts (skinless, boneless)	180°C	15–20 mins	75°C	Turn halfway
Thighs (skinless, boneless)	180°C	15 mins	75°C	Turn halfway
Wings	180°C	25 mins	75°C	Turn halfway
Legs	180°C	30–35 mins	75°C	Turn halfway
Drumsticks	180°C	25 mins	75°C	Turn halfway

Pork

INGREDIENT	AIR FRYER TEMP	TIME	INTERNAL FOOD TEMP	NOTES
Shoulder joint	180°C	15 mins per 450g	63°C	Rind-side down for 1 hour, then 20 mins rind-side up
Gammon joint (approx. 1.5kg)	180°C	1 hour	68°C	Turn halfway
Bacon	180°C	8 mins	Until crisp	Turn halfway
Sausages	180°C	10 mins	68°C	Turn halfway
Pork chops	180°C	30–35 mins	75°C	Turn halfway

Beef

INGREDIENT	AIR FRYER TEMP	TIME	INTERNAL FOOD TEMP	NOTES
Roasting joint	180°C	15 mins per 450g (rare) +10 mins (medium) +20 mins (well-done)	52°C (rare) 63°C (medium) 71°C (well-done)	Turn halfway
Steak (approx. 250g)	200°C	8 mins (rare) 10 mins (medium) 12 mins (well-done)	52°C (rare) 63°C (medium) 71°C (well-done)	Turn halfway
Burgers	180°C	10 mins	71°C	Turn halfway

Lamb

INGREDIENT	AIR FRYER TEMP	TIME	INTERNAL FOOD TEMP	NOTES
Roasting joint	180°C	20 mins per 450g (medium) +10 mins (well-done)	63°C (medium) 71°C (well-done)	Turn halfway
Chops (bone-in)	180°C	12 mins	63°C	Turn halfway
Steaks (bone-in)	180°C	12–15 mins	63°C	Turn halfway
Burgers	180°C	10 mins	63°C	Turn halfway
Kofta	180°C	8–10 mins	63°C	Turn halfway

Fish

INGREDIENT	AIR FRYER TEMP	TIME	INTERNAL FOOD TEMP	NOTES
Salmon fillets	180°C	12 mins	63°C	Turn halfway
Cod fillets	180°C	12–15 mins	63°C	Turn halfway
King Prawns	180°C	4 mins	63°C	Turn halfway
Fish cakes	180°C	10–12 mins	63°C	Turn halfway
Fish fingers (from frozen)	180°C	12 mins	63°C	Turn halfway

Potatoes

INGREDIENT	AIR FRYER TEMP	TIME	INTERNAL FOOD TEMP	NOTES
Jacket potatoes	200°C	45 mins	Until fluffy	Spray with oil, turn halfway
Roast potatoes	200°C	30 mins	Until crisp	Parboil for 5 mins, drain and spray with oil, shake basket halfway
Wedges	180°C	25 mins	Until crisp	Shake basket halfway
Chips	180°C	25 mins	Until crisp	Shake basket halfway
Oven chips (chunky, from frozen)	180°C	20 mins	Until crisp	Shake basket halfway
Oven chips (fine, from frozen)	180°C	15–20 mins	Until crisp	Shake basket halfway

About the Recipes

The recipes in this book have all been tried and tested in my home kitchen. Lockdown had very few upsides, but one was that it gave me the opportunity to explore my love for creating delicious, affordable and simple family meals. You'll see that a lot of the recipes use leftovers from the fridge – this is because I wanted them to be as adaptable and low-waste as possible. If you have leftovers or slightly left-field ingredients, then use them. You might even make the dish better! The same applies to levels of spice; if you like things hot then feel free to ramp it up and, likewise, if you prefer things mild then reduce or omit them altogether. There is no right or wrong way to cook them!

You'll notice that most of the recipes in the book are designed to serve two. This is because most air fryers will easily cook a meal of this size and I wanted the recipes to be useful to everyone. If you have a larger air fryer and are catering for a bigger crowd then simply double the recipe and you're good to go.

The timings that I've given are for guidance only and I do urge you to use a thermometer to make sure that everything is cooked through – especially if you're just getting started and aren't used to your air fryer. What cooks in 15 minutes in my fryer, may only take 12 or 13 minutes in yours. Much like a normal oven, some run hotter than others, but you'll get to know the quirks of your machine the more you use it.

You may use the recipes in this book every day or perhaps only a handful will make it into your repertoire, or you'll use the information in this front section as inspiration to create your own. Whatever you use it for, I do hope it will inspire you to embrace this new way of cooking. Air fryers aren't complicated to use, but they are different to what many of us are used to, so just take time getting used to yours and finding out what works best. I hope you enjoy making these recipes as much I did. Once you've started cooking, do give me a tag on Instagram @airfryeruk – I would so love to see what you create in yours!

Rec

pes

Breakfast & Brunch

Start your day right!

All-in-One Weekend Brunch

PREP 5 minutes   **COOK** 10–15 minutes   **SERVES** 1   **KIT** Heatproof dish that fits in your air fryer

This is a brilliantly simple brunch that is all built and cooked in one go in the air fryer. It makes a generous breakfast or brunch for one person, but can also be bulked out with toast and split happily between two.

1 medium potato, peeled and
    finely sliced into discs
1 tsp English mustard powder
4 tbsp milk
100g fresh spinach, washed
130g diced chorizo
80g Cheddar cheese, grated
2 eggs
olive oil, for spraying
sea salt and freshly ground black
    pepper

1. Spray your dish with a little olive oil, then arrange the potato discs in a single layer in the base of the dish. Sprinkle over the mustard powder and pour over the milk. Cover the potatoes with the spinach in an even layer, then scatter over the chopped chorizo. Top with the grated Cheddar, then crack both eggs over and season generously with salt and pepper.

2. Transfer the dish to the air fryer and cook at 180°C for 10–15 minutes, checking every 5 minutes, until everything is cooked through and the cheese is bubbling. Serve hot.

Breakfast Muffins

PREP 5 minutes   **COOK** 20 minutes   **MAKES** 4   **KIT** 4 silicone cupcake cases

These tasty muffins make a great grab-and-go breakfast. They can be eaten hot or cold, so make them ahead for those days when you know you'll be rushed off your feet in the morning. This recipe is really easy to scale up, so make double or triple the amount if you've got lots of hungry mouths to feed.

8 rashers pancetta
4 eggs
80g Cheddar cheese, grated
sea salt and freshly ground black
   pepper
tomato ketchup, for dipping
   (optional)

1. Lay the rashers of pancetta in the base of the air fryer in a single layer, making sure not to overlap them. Cook at 190°C for 5 minutes, until crisp, checking halfway through the cooking time and turning the rashers if necessary, until crisp on all sides.

2. Crack the eggs into a bowl, season with salt and pepper and beat to combine. Add the grated cheese to the bowl and beat again.

3. Once the pancetta has finished cooking, snip or crumble it into small pieces.

4. Add half of the pancetta to the bowl with the eggs and cheese and stir to incorporate, then evenly divide the mixture between the silicone cupcake cases and scatter the remaining pancetta over the top.

5. Transfer the filled cupcake cases to the air fryer and cook at 180°C for 15 minutes, checking occasionally, until the muffins are cooked through. Serve warm or cold with ketchup alongside for dipping.

Speedy Breakfast Omelette

PREP 5 minutes **COOK** 18 minutes **SERVES** 1 **KIT** Large, round silicone mould

Omelettes are so easy and adaptable that they make the perfect meal at any time of day. I've suggested tomatoes, peppers and onions here, but you can use any filling that suits your mood. This is a two-egg omelette that feeds one, but you could scale it up if you're cooking for two or more, just make sure the eggs are set all the way through before serving.

4 cherry tomatoes, halved
½ red or yellow pepper, deseeded
    and roughly chopped
½ red onion, peeled and sliced
2 tsp olive oil
2 eggs, beaten
25g grated Cheddar cheese
sea salt and freshly ground black
    pepper

1. Put the tomatoes, pepper and onion in the silicone mould and add the oil. Give everything a stir to ensure the vegetables are coated in the oil, then transfer to the air fryer and cook at 180°C for 5 minutes, until the vegetables are almost tender.

2. Add the beaten eggs and a generous grinding of salt and pepper to the mould and stir to evenly distribute the vegetables. Return to the air fryer and cook for 8 minutes, until the omelette is almost cooked. Scatter over the cheese and cook for an additional 5 minutes, until the cheese is melted and golden and the omelette is cooked through.

3. Turn the omelette out onto a serving plate and serve immediately.

Speedy Fry-Up

PREP 5 minutes   **COOK** 10 minutes   **SERVES** 1 (double-up if you have a larger air fryer)
KIT 3 silicone cupcake cases or heatproof ceramic ramekins

A cooked breakfast at the weekend is a real treat but can leave you with a messy kitchen when you just want to put your feet up with a cup of tea and read the papers. Aside from the toast, this is all made in the air fryer, cutting down on the mess and making it just that little bit healthier, too!

2 eggs
4 cherry tomatoes, halved
3 rashers pancetta
olive oil, for spraying
sea salt and freshly ground
    pepper
buttered toast, to serve (optional)

1. Spray the silicone cupcake cases or ramekins with a little olive oil. Crack an egg each into the first 2 moulds or ramekins, then fill the third with the tomatoes. Season all 3 with salt and pepper, then spray the tomatoes with a little more olive oil.

2. Place the moulds or ramekins containing the eggs and tomatoes in the base of the air fryer and cook at 180°C for 5 minutes, then open the fryer and lay the pancetta slices in the base in an even layer. While the fryer is open, check your eggs – if you like a soft yolk, they may be done already, but make sure the whites are fully cooked through.

3. Close the fryer and cook at the same temperature for another 5 minutes, checking the eggs and pancetta occasionally, until everything is cooked to your liking. Serve hot, on freshly buttered toast, if you like.

Celeriac Rösti with Fried Eggs

PREP 10 minutes   **COOK** 20 minutes   **SERVES** 2

I've put this recipe in the brunch section, but it would also make a delicious lunch or light dinner, especially when drizzled in a little chilli sauce. If you have a larger air fryer, you could cook your eggs at the same time as your rösti – simply crack them into a lightly oiled silicone mould and add to the fryer for the last 5 minutes of cooking time.

½ large celeriac, peeled and grated

3 medium potatoes, peeled and grated

1 white onion, finely chopped

1 tsp cumin seeds

4 eggs, beaten

sea salt and freshly ground black pepper

rocket leaves, to serve (optional)

1. Pile the grated celeriac and potatoes in the centre of a clean tea towel, then bring up the edges and twist tightly over a sink to enclose the grated veg and squeeze out as much moisture as possible. Tip the contents of the tea towel into a bowl.

2. Add the chopped onion, cumin seeds, beaten eggs and a generous grinding of salt and pepper to the bowl with the grated vegetables and stir everything until well combined.

3. Lay a sheet of baking paper that will fit in the base of your air fryer on the kitchen counter. Divide the celeriac and potato mixture into halves or quarters (depending on whether you want 2 large or 4 smaller fritters) and form into round fritters on the prepared baking paper (I like to press mine down slightly with a baking sheet to get them nice and flat).

4. Carefully transfer the baking paper to the air fryer and cook for 20 minutes at 180°C, flipping the röstis halfway through the cooking time. Check the röstis every 5 minutes or so and remove them when the are crisp and golden – if you have opted to make smaller röstis, they will cook quicker than larger ones.

5. When the röstis are almost cooked, fry the eggs to your liking and prepare a rocket salad to serve alongside, if you like. Serve the röstis hot, topped with the fried eggs and with the salad alongside.

Granola

PREP 5 minutes   **COOK** 15 minutes   **MAKES** 1 small jar   **KIT** Heatproof dish that fits in your air fryer

Topped with fresh fruit and doused in yoghurt or milk, granola is a great way to start the day. This makes a fairly small portion, but you can scale it up if you want to make more – just need to bear in mind the size of your air fryer and cook the granola in batches if necessary. Kept in an airtight jar, this will keep for up to one month.

1 tbsp vegetable oil
3 tbsp maple syrup
2 tbsp peanut butter (smooth or crunchy)
200g rolled oats
25g pumpkin seeds
25g chopped walnuts
50g flaked almonds
25g coconut flakes
25g dried cranberries
yoghurt, fresh berries and honey, to serve (optional)

1. Line your heatproof dish with baking paper and set to one side while you prepare the granola.

2. In a large bowl, combine the vegetable oil, maple syrup and peanut butter, then tip in the oats, pumpkin seeds, chopped walnuts and flaked almonds, then stir again until everything is well coated.

3. Tip the mixture into your prepared dish, spreading it out evenly, then transfer to the air fryer and cook at 180°C for 10 minutes.

4. After 10 minutes, open the air fryer, add the coconut flakes and cranberries and give the granola a stir. Cook for another 5 minutes at 180°C, then set aside to cool.

5. Serve the granola with yoghurt, fresh fruit and a squeeze of honey, if you like, or store in an airtight container for up to 1 month.

Avocado & Feta Breakfast Bruschetta

PREP 5 minutes   **COOK** 8 minutes   **SERVES** 2

This hybrid between a bruschetta and a classic avocado on toast makes a wonderful breakfast or light lunch and is ready in less than 10 minutes, meaning that it's not just for weekends. I like mine scattered with fresh chilli but you can leave that off if you're not a fan of heat.

1 ciabatta roll
1 ripe avocado, peeled, halved
    and stone removed
2 ripe tomatoes, thinly sliced
100g feta cheese, crumbled
1 red chilli, thinly sliced
a handful of fresh basil leaves
olive oil, for spraying
sea salt and freshly ground black
    pepper

1. Slice off the top half of the ciabatta roll, then cut each half into 2 equal pieces.

2. Put the avocado flesh in a bowl, season with salt and pepper and mash with a fork to the consistency of your choice. Spread the avocado over the cut-sides of the ciabatta pieces.

3. Top each piece of ciabatta with a few sliced tomatoes, then crumble over the feta cheese and spray each with a little of the olive oil.

4. Place the bruschettas in the air fryer and cook at 180°C for 8 minutes, until the bread is crisp and the feta is golden.

5. Divide the bruschettas between 2 serving plates, scatter with sliced chilli and torn basil leaves, then serve.

Lunches & Light Meals

Get out of the sandwich rut!

Chicken Satay

PREP 5 minutes   **COOK** 15 minutes   **SERVES** 2
KIT Wooden skewers, soaked in water for at least 30 minutes

This classic dish of skewers of juicy chicken dressed in a lightly spiced peanut sauce is the perfect thing to serve for a light lunch or with drinks as an informal dinner party starter. The wooden skewers will be fine in the air fryer, but to prevent them from charring it is a good idea to soak them in water for 30 minutes or so before cooking.

2 skinless, boneless chicken breasts, cut into bite-sized pieces
sea salt and freshly ground black pepper

For the satay sauce:

3 tbsp smooth peanut butter (chunky is fine if you already have it to hand)
1 tbsp soy sauce
juice of ½ lime
1 tsp runny honey
200ml coconut milk
1 tsp curry powder

1. Slide the chunks of chicken onto the wooden skewers so that you have 4–5 pieces on each one. Season with salt and pepper and lay in the base of your air fryer in a single layer. Cook at 200°C for 15 minutes, until the chicken is tender and cooked through.

2. While the chicken is cooking, make the satay sauce by heating the peanut butter in a small pan over a medium heat. Once hot, add the soy sauce, lime juice, honey, coconut milk and curry powder and continue to cook, stirring continuously, until heated through, smooth and glossy.

3. Divide the satay sauce between 2 serving bowls and serve with the chicken skewers alongside for dipping and drizzling.

Goat's Cheese & Caramelised Onion Tarts

PREP 10 minutes **COOK** 15 minutes **MAKES** 4–6 **KIT** 6 silicone cupcake cases

These classy little tarts make the perfect light lunch when served with salad, but would also be wonderful as canapés for a party. They can be assembled really quickly from just a handful of ingredients, making them the perfect option for fuss-free entertaining. I use store-bought caramelised onion chutney for ease, though, if you have a bit more time, you could cook some onions down slowly until sticky and sweet and use those instead.

1 sheet pre-rolled puff pastry
1 jar caramelised onion chutney or marmalade
1 log soft goat's cheese (around 125g), crumbled
1 egg, beaten
sea salt and freshly ground black pepper
salad leave and balsamic glaze, to serve (optional)

1. Unroll the puff pastry sheet on its baking-paper backing and stamp out small rounds using a 9 cm/3½ inch round cutter, rerolling and cutting any scraps of pastry until it is all used up.

2. Press the puff pastry rounds into the silicone cupcake cases so that edges of the pastry come up the sides of the cases.

3. Put a teaspoon of the caramelised onion mixture in the base of each of the pastry-filled cases, then top with a layer of crumbled goat's cheese. Repeat the layers twice so that each tart has three layers of onion and three layers of goat's cheese.

4. Transfer the filled cases to the air fryer and cook at 180°C for 8–10 minutes, until the pastry is crisp and the cheese is golden and bubbling.

5. Transfer the tarts to a serving platter or individual plates and serve hot, with salad and balsamic glaze alongside, if you like.

Honey & Parsnip Soup

PREP 10 minutes **COOK** 20 minutes **SERVES** 2
KIT Heatproof dish that fits in your air fryer

Making soup in the air fryer might seem like a stretch but it is perfect for quickly roasting veg and then blending to a warming soup with some stock. This parsnip and honey soup is earthy, sweet and delicious – perfect for cold autumn days. Once made, this will keep in the fridge for up to five days.

3 parsnips, peeled and roughly sliced
1 tbsp vegetable oil
1 small white onion, peeled and roughly sliced
1 small carrot, peeled and roughly sliced
2 garlic cloves, peeled
2 tbsp runny honey
1 tsp dried rosemary
600ml vegetable stock
4 tbsp double cream
sea salt and freshly ground black pepper
crusty bread, to serve (optional)

1. Put the parsnips and olive oil in your heatproof dish and toss to coat. Transfer the dish to the air fryer and cook at 160°C for 10 minutes.

2. Once the parsnips are part-cooked, open the air fryer and add the onion, carrot, garlic cloves, honey and dried rosemary to the dish and stir to combine. Cook for another 10 minutes at 160°C, until all the vegetables are tender.

3. Transfer the cooked veg to the jug of a blender along with the vegetable stock, double cream and a generous grinding of salt and pepper. Blend until smooth.

4. Spoon the soup into bowls and serve the hot, with crusty bread alongside for dunking, if you like.

Tomato & Basil Soup

PREP 10 minutes   **COOK** 15 minutes   **SERVES** 2
KIT Heatproof dish that fits in your air fryer

This is a great recipe to use up the abundance of summer tomatoes. It's so quick to make and keeps in the fridge in an airtight container for up to five days, and once cooled you can freeze it too. If you make it a little thicker, it also makes a delicious pasta sauce.

4 large ripe tomatoes, sliced
1 small red onion, sliced
2 garlic cloves
a good glug of olive oil
1 tsp Worcestershire sauce
a handful of basil leaves
vegetable stock (optional)
sea salt and freshly ground black
    pepper

To serve:
crusty bread
grated Parmesan cheese

1. Put the sliced tomatoes and onion into your heatproof dish, along with the garlic. Drizzle over a glug of olive oil and season generously with salt and pepper. Transfer the dish to your air fryer and cook at 160°C for 10 minutes. Give the mixture a stir and return it to the fryer for a further 5 minutes.

2. Carefully remove your dish from the fryer and tip the contents into a blender or smoothie maker. Add your Worcestershire sauce and fresh basil and blend until you have a soup consistency. You may need to add some vegetable stock at this point, depending on how juicy your tomatoes were and how thick or thin you like your soup. Taste and add more seasoning if it needs it.

3. Pour the soup into bowls and serve with some crusty bread and a sprinkle of grated Parmesan on the top.

Spicy Corn Fritters

PREP 10 minutes   **COOK** 15 minutes   **SERVES** 2 as a light lunch
KIT 1 large silicone mould (optional)

I love these fritters – they are really tasty, perfect for making with the kids and, if you're lucky enough to have leftovers, can be easily reheated the next day and are just as delicious. My family like a bit of spice, but if yours aren't keen then feel free to omit or lessen the amount chilli. Using a silicone mould isn't strictly necessary but will help keep your air fryer clean and save on some tricky washing up, which I am always a fan of!

1 x 200g can sweetcorn, drained
5 spring onions, trimmed and
    thinly sliced
1 tbsp olive oil
1 egg, beaten
1 red chilli, finely sliced, or to taste
60g plain flour
1 tsp baking powder
1 small bunch fresh parsley, leaves
    picked and chopped
sea salt and freshly ground black
    pepper

For the sriracha mayo:

2 tbsp mayonnaise
2 tsp sriracha sauce, or to taste

1. In a large mixing bowl, combine the sweetcorn, spring onions and chilli. Add the olive oil and beaten egg and stir to combine.

2. Sift the flour and baking powder into the bowl and season with a generous grinding of salt and pepper. Stir everything until well combined.

3. Line your silicone mould or the base of your air fryer with baking paper. Use your hands to form small handfuls of the mixture into round patties. Lay the patties on the baking paper and repeat until all of the mixture is used up Depending on the size of your air fryer, you may need to do this in batches.

4. Cook at 180°C for 15 minutes, turning the fritters halfway through the cooking time, until crisp and golden.

5. While the fritters are cooking, make the spicy mayo dip by combining the mayonnaise and sriracha in a small bowl.

6. Serve the fritters hot, garnished with freshly chopped parsley, additional sliced chilli and with the sriracha mayo alongside for dipping.

Spicy Paprika Prawn Skewers

PREP 10 minutes, plus marinating   **COOK** 8–10 minutes   **SERVES** 2
KIT Wooden skewers, soaked in water for at least 30 minutes

If I'm being organised, I like to marinate my prawns the night before I'm planning to serve this, but it's not a problem at all to do it maybe an hour before if time doesn't permit – they will still be super flavoursome.

165g raw king prawns
1 red pepper, deseeded and
    chopped into squares
1 garlic clove, peeled and grated
1 red chilli, finely diced, plus extra
    to taste
1 tsp paprika
1 lime
olive oil spray
sea salt and freshly ground black
    pepper

To serve:

2 mini tortilla wraps
a bag of watercress

1. In a large bowl, combine the prawns, red pepper, garlic, chilli and paprika. Juice half of the lime and add the juice to the bowl, then season with salt and pepper. Mix everything together, making sure to coat all the prawns and red pepper with the flavourings. If you like it a little spicier add a little more chilli – always adjust the ingredients to your preferred tastes. Leave to marinate in the fridge for at least an hour, or even overnight.

2. When you're ready to cook, slide your prawns and pepper pieces onto wooden skewers, alternating between the two. Spray the skewers with a little oil and place them into your air fryer. Cook at 180°C for 8–10 minutes, until cooked through and browning. All air fryers tend to be a little different, so do always check during cooking and adjust the cooking time accordingly.

3. Serve the skewers on mini tortilla wraps with watercress salad. Squeeze the remaining lime half over the skewers for an added bite.

Mini Crustless Quiches

PREP 5 minutes   **COOK** 10 minutes   **SERVES** 4
KIT 4 heatproof ceramic ramekins or large silicone cupcake cases

These are halfway between a quiche and a kind of baked omelette and are a brilliant lunchtime option for when you have eggs and an array of veg to use up in the fridge. I've suggested a filling combination below, but feel free to mix it up and use whatever you have to hand. Ham, chorizo, courgettes or spinach would all be welcome additions!

4 eggs
80g Cheddar cheese, grated
1 tbsp chopped parsley
100g purple sprouting broccoli, roughly chopped
sea salt and freshly ground black pepper
spinach and watercress salad, to serve (optional)

1. Crack the eggs into a large bowl and beat to combine. Add the cheese, parsley and a generous grinding of salt and pepper and beat again.

2. Divide the chopped broccoli (or other filling ingredients) between the ramekins or silicone cases, then pour over the egg and cheese mixture to fill.

3. Place the ramekins or silicone cases in the air fryer and cook at 190°C for 10 minutes, until the egg mixture is cooked through. If the egg is still soft in the middle, cook the quiches for an additional 5 minutes, until firm.

4. If you have cooked the quiches in ramekins, serve them in the dishes, otherwise turn out onto serving plates and serve hot, with spinach and watercress salad alongside.

Homemade Fish Fingers

PREP 10 minutes   **COOK** 10–12 minutes   **SERVES** 2

Every parent's saviour, here the humble fish finger has been elevated to make for a very special lunch indeed. Slightly stale bread is great for this, though panko breadcrumbs also work brilliantly if you have some to hand.

2 fillets skinless, boneless cod (approx. 150g each)
3 slices bread (slightly stale is fine)
60g plain flour
2 eggs
sea salt and freshly ground black pepper

For fish finger sandwiches:

1 crusty baguette
butter
mayonnaise
watercress
1 lemon, for squeezing

1. Lay the cod fillets on a board, pat dry with kitchen paper and season on both sides with a little salt and pepper. Slice the fillets into 'fingers'. (These can be slightly larger than the store-bought variety – I usually aim for 3–4 out of each fillet.)

2. Put your bread and a generous grinding of salt and pepper in a food processor or blender and blitz to fine crumbs.

3. Set 3 shallow bowls on your work surface. Put the flour in the first, beat the eggs into the second and put the seasoned breadcrumbs in the third.

4. Working with one finger of fish at a time, dip the fish first in the flour to coat, then in the egg, then in the breadcrumbs, making sure they are fully coated at each stage.

5. Lay the fingers in the base of the air fryer and repeat until all of the fish has been coated.

6. Cook the fish fingers at 190°C for 10–12 minutes, turning halfway through, until the crust is golden and the fish is cooked through. (If you have an instant-read thermometer, you are aiming for an internal temperature of 63°C.)

7. If you are making fish finger sandwiches, while the fish fingers are cooking slice the baguette in half, then cut open each half baguette. Spread the rolls with butter and mayonnaise, then fill with fresh watercress. Arrange the cooked fish fingers over the top, squeeze over a little lemon juice and serve immediately.

Breaded Prawns with Garlic Mayo

PREP 10 minutes   **COOK** 8 minutes   **SERVES** 2   **KIT** 1 large silicone mould (optional)

This favourite starter is so quick to make with an air fryer and the quick cooking ensures the prawns remain plump and juicy inside whilst still getting that golden and crisp coat. Serve with a punchy homemade garlic mayo dip.

60g panko breadcrumbs
8 large prawns, shelled but tails
    left on
60g plain flour
1 egg, beaten
1 tsp garlic powder
1 tsp paprika
sea salt and freshly ground black
    pepper

For the garlic mayo:
2 heaped tbsp mayonnaise
2 garlic cloves, grated
a squeeze of lemon juice

1. Set up a production line: put your flour into a shallow bowl and mix in the garlic powder, paprika and salt and pepper to taste. Put the beaten egg in another bowl and put the panko breadcrumbs onto a plate.

2. Coat each prawn first in the flour, followed by the egg, then finally in the panko breadcrumbs, making sure they are well coated at each stage. When all of the prawns are covered, place them into your air fryer, either directly into the basket or use a liner, making sure they don't overlap. Cook at 190°C for 5–8 minutes, depending on the size of your prawns, until cooked through and golden.

3. While your prawns are cooking, prepare your garlic mayonnaise. Put the mayonnaise in a small bowl and add your grated garlic and lemon juice. Season to taste and serve alongside the cooked prawns.

Loaded Potato Skins

PREP 10 minutes   **COOK** 40 minutes   **SERVES** 2

This is a great way to breathe new life into those potatoes that you have languishing at the back of the fridge that need using up. To make these veggie, just omit the chorizo, though you could add a pinch of paprika to the potato mixture if you are craving a bit of smoky spice.

4 medium potatoes, halved
olive oil, for spraying
80g Cheddar cheese, grated
12 slices chorizo
4 cherry tomatoes, sliced
1 small red onion, thinly sliced
2 tbsp sour cream, to serve
chopped chives, to garnish

1. Put the potato halves in the air fryer, cut-side up. Spray lightly with olive oil, then cook at 180°C for 20–30 minutes, until the potato flesh is soft and the skin is crisp. Set aside until cool enough to handle.

2. Once slightly cooled, scoop out the potato flesh from the skins and add to a bowl. Mash the potato flesh lightly with a fork, then add the chorizo slices and half of the cheese and stir to combine.

3. Scoop half of the mixture back into the potato skins and level out, then add a layer of sliced tomatoes and a layer of onion. Top with the remaining potato, then add the rest of the cheese.

4. Put the filled potato skins in the air fryer and cook at 180°C for 5–8 minutes, until the cheese is golden and bubbling.

5. Divide the potato skins between serving plates and serve with a dollop of soured cream and a scattering of chopped chives alongside.

Pizza Bagels

PREP 5 minutes   **COOK** 5 minutes   **SERVES** 2

With all the flavour of pizza, these simple bagels will be a hit with kids and grown-ups alike. If you are making these with children, get them to dress their own and use up any veg that you have in the fridge. I've suggested a simple topping of red pesto, mozzarella and chorizo here, but tomatoes, peppers and sweetcorn would all be welcome additions, so feel free to colour outside of the lines!

2 bagels, halved
1 tbsp red pesto
a handful of fresh basil leaves
80g grated mozzarella cheese
70g sliced chorizo
1 tsp chilli oil

1. Lay the bagels on a board, cut sides up. Spread each half bagel with half a tablespoon of pesto, then scatter over some of the basil leaves. Divide the cheese between the bagels, then top each with some of the chorizo slices.

2. Transfer the pizza bagels to the base of the air fryer and cook at 180°C for 5 minutes, until the cheese is golden and bubbling and the chorizo is cooked through. (You may need to do this in batches if you have a smaller air fryer.)

3. Transfer the bagels to serving plates, scatter with the remaining basil leaves and drizzle with a little chilli oil before serving.

Pastry Pizza Tarts

PREP 10 minutes   **COOK** 10 minutes   **SERVES** 2   **KIT** Baking paper

These are such quick and simple lunch and are perfect served with salad. I don't use the balls of mozzarella, as I find they can be watery and will create a soggy base – instead, look for the dryer blocks of "pizza mozzarella" or the packs of ready-grated cheese.

½ pack puff pastry
plain flour, for dusting
2 tsp pesto
120g grated mozzarella
6 slices chorizo, chopped
3–5 sundried tomatoes, chopped
1 tsp dried oregano
1 egg, beaten
a handful of fresh basil, chopped

To serve:
rocket and watercress salad
chilli oil

1. Roll out the puff pastry on a flour-dusted surface and slice in half to make two rectangles. Place each rectangle onto a piece of baking paper, then fold the four edges in to create a small barrier to contain your toppings.

2. Spread the base of each tart with 1 teaspoon of the red pesto, giving an even coverage. Scatter over your grated mozzarella and your chorizo. Finish with your chopped sun-dried tomatoes and oregano.

3. Brush the edges of the pasty with beaten egg before placing the tarts carefully into the air fryer – either on baking paper or straight into the fryer. Cook at 190°C for 10 minutes until the pastry is cooked and they are golden.

4. When the tarts are ready, sprinkle over your chopped fresh basil and serve with a watercress and rocket salad and a drizzle of chilli oil.

Salmon on Rye, with Soft Cheese & Chives

PREP 10 minutes   **COOK** 20 minutes   **SERVES** 2   **KIT** 1 large silicone mould

Nutty rye bread, creamy soft cheese and tender salmon make such a good combo, and can be easily whipped up for a satisfying Sunday brunch.

2 slices rye bread
1 lemon, sliced
2 salmon fillets
2 tbsp soft cheese
a few chives, snipped
sea salt and freshly ground black
   pepper

1. Start by placing the rye bread slices in your air fryer. Cook at 200°C for 3 minutes, then remove and set aside. (You can also toast the bread in a toaster, if preferred.)

2. Place your lemon slices in the base of a large silicone mould and pop your salmon fillets on top. Set your air fryer to 180°C and cook the salmon for 15 minutes, or until cooked and opaque throughout.

3. Spread each of your toasted rye bread slices with a tablespoon of soft cheese. When the salmon is ready, remove it from the fryer and flake it onto your toast. Sprinkle the chives over the tops of the toasts, season to taste and enjoy.

Salmon & Spring Onion Fishcakes

PREP 10 minutes **COOK** 10 minutes **SERVES** 2–4

Fishcakes are a great option for a quick midweek lunch or dinner. I've used salmon here, but you could use tinned tuna instead if you prefer. If you can't get hold of ready-cooked salmon fillets or would prefer to cook your own, simply air fry the raw salmon for 15 minutes at 180°C before starting the recipe.

2 cooked salmon fillets (if cooking from raw, see recipe intro)

1 bunch spring onions, finely chopped

½ tsp paprika

45g panko breadcrumbs

1 large egg, beaten

juice and zest of 1 lemon

4 tbsp mayonnaise

handful of fresh parsley, leaves chopped

sea salt and freshly ground black pepper

green salad, to serve

1. Remove and discard any salmon skin, then flake your cooked salmon fillets into a large bowl. Add the spring onions, paprika, panko breadcrumbs, beaten egg, lemon zest, half of the lemon juice, 2 tablespoons of the mayonnaise, most of the chopped parsley and a generous grinding of salt and pepper, then give everything a good stir until well combined.

2. Divide the mixture into 4 equal portions, then form each portion into a round patty with your hand. Place in the base of the air fryer and cook at 190°C for 10 minutes, turning halfway through.

3. While the fishcakes are cooking, make a lemon and parsley mayonnaise by combining the remaining 2 tablespoons of mayonnaise with the remaining lemon juice and parsley.

4. Transfer the cooked fishcakes to serving plates and serve with the lemon and parsley mayo and some green salad alongside.

Mini Open Veggie Sausage Pies

PREP 20 minutes   **COOK** 15 minutes   **MAKES** 4–6
KIT 10cm cookie cutter and small silicone cupcake moulds

Easy party food or for a picnic, or anytime! I defrost my sausages the night before and chop them up into smaller pieces.

1 sheet pre-rolled puff pastry
plain flour, for dusting
olive oil spray
chutney of your choice
3 veggie sausages, roughly
   chopped
1 egg, beaten

1. Roll out the puff pastry on a flour-dusted surface, and stamp out 10cm circles using the cookie cutter. Reroll the pastry and repeat until it is all used up. Spray your moulds with a little olive oil so the pastry does not stick, then place the pastry circles into your moulds and press them down so they fit snugly and come up the sides.

2. Place a teaspoon of your chosen chutney in the base of each pastry cup. Top with the chopped sausages, dividing them equally between the cups. Brush each cup with the egg wash.

3. Pop the little cups into your air fryer and cook at 180°C for around 15 minutes, checking halfway through cooking, until the pastry is crisp and golden and the sausages are cooked. You may need to cook them in batches, depending on the size of your air fryer.

Pears with Feta & Beetroot

PREP 5 minutes   **COOK** 20 minutes   **SERVES** 2

Sweet, salty and earthy, these flavours complement each other so well and combine to create a light lunch or starter that feels really special but can be put together really quickly. If you are making this for a starter, half a pear will be enough for each person, so this recipe could happily feed four.

2 pears, peeled, halved lengthways and cores removed
1 cooked and peeled beetroot, grated
100g feta cheese, crumbled
balsamic vinegar, for drizzling
rocket salad, to serve (optional)

1. Lay the pears in the base of the air fryer, cored-side up, then divide the grated beetroot and crumbled feta between the pears, filling the cavity where the cores have been removed.

2. Cook at 160°C for 20 minutes, until the pears are soft and the cheese is golden.

3. Divide the pears between serving plates and drizzle with a little balsamic vinegar. Serve with a rocket salad alongside.

Stuffed Courgettes

PREP 15 minutes **COOK** 20 minutes **SERVES** 2–4

This is great as a little side dish to accompany any meal, or for two people as a light lunch. You can make it vegan too by replacing the cheese with a vegan substitute.

2 courgettes
4 sun-dried tomatoes, finely
   chopped
120g grated mozzarella
a handful of fresh basil leaves,
   chopped
1 fresh chilli, chopped
sea salt and freshly ground black
   pepper

1. Cut your courgettes in half lengthways, scoop out the middle with a tablespoon and add to a bowl. Finely chop your sun-dried tomatoes and add them to the courgette flesh along with the chopped basil and chilli. Season with salt and pepper, then use the mixture to fill your courgette boats. Sprinkle the mozzarella over the tops of the courgettes.

2. Transfer the filled courgettes to the air fryer and cook at 160°C for about 20 minutes, depending on the size of your courgettes, until the courgette is tender, the cheese is melted and the top is golden.

Beef Tomatoes Stuffed with Veggie Couscous

PREP 20 minutes   **COOK** 20 minutes   **SERVES** 2   **KIT** Large silicone liner

These stuffed tomatoes make for a really vibrant lunch and are perfect for the warmer months when you have a glut of tomatoes on your hands that need using up. These would also make a wonderfully fresh starter for an al fresco dinner party.

2 beef tomatoes
150g couscous
1 vegetable stock cube
1 tbsp olive oil
1 small red onion, finely diced
1 small yellow pepper, deseeded and diced
½ tsp paprika
½ tsp garlic granules
2 tbsp finely chopped flat leaf parsley
a handful of panko breadcrumbs
sea salt and freshly ground black pepper

To serve:
mixed green salad
1 tsp pine nuts
balsamic vinegar, for drizzling

1. Cut the tops off the beef tomatoes by cutting around the stalk working on an angle, remove the tomato stem from each tomato, leaving about a 2cm gap around the edge. With a spoon, scoop out the insides of the tomatoes – I save the insides for a soup or pasta sauce later.

2. Make up the couscous according to the packet instructions, dissolving the stock in the hot water first. Set aside, covered, to soak.

3. Meanwhile, add the oil to a frying pan and fry your onions and pepper for 5 minutes until softening. Add the paprika and garlic powder and cook for a couple more minutes, then season to taste.

4. Fluff up the couscous with a fork, then add the vegetable mixture to the couscous, along with the chopped parsley and stir everything together. Divide the filling between the two hollowed out tomatoes, then top each with half of the panko crumbs.

5. Place your tomatoes in a large silicone liner and transfer to your air fryer. Cook at 180°C for 15 minutes until hot throughout and the crumbs are golden. Remove the tomatoes carefully from the fryer and serve with a crisp green salad, a scatter of pine nuts and a drizzle of balsamic vinegar.

Mains

Hearty meals for the whole family!

Spicy Chicken Goujons

PREP 10 minutes   **COOK** 20 minutes   **SERVES** 2   **KIT** Baking paper

These are such a favourite in my house and are the number one thing that my son asks me to make when he has his friends over from school. I use spicy tortilla chips for the coating for an extra punch of flavour, but if you prefer things milder then swap them out for a plainer variety.

2 skinless, boneless chicken breasts
1 large pack spicy tortilla chips (I like Dorito's Chilli Heatwave)
2 tsp chilli powder
120g plain flour
2 eggs
sea salt and freshly ground black pepper
sauces, wraps and salad, to serve (optional)

1. Lay the chicken breasts on a chopping board and slice into long strips. Set aside.
2. To make the goujon coating, crush the tortilla chips until fine – you can do this in the bag by bashing with a rolling pin or by tipping the tortilla chips into a food processor and pulsing until you have fine crumbs. Tip the crumbs into a large bowl.
3. Set 2 additional bowl on the work surface then put the flour and chilli powder in the first bowl and stir to combine. Crack the eggs into the second bowl and beat to combine.
4. Working with one piece of chicken at a time, dip the goujons first in the flour mixture, then in the egg, then in the crushed tortilla chips, thoroughly coating the chicken at each stage.
5. Line the base of your air fryer with baking paper, then lay the coated goujons on the paper in a single layer.
6. Once all of the goujons are coated, cook in the air fryer at 180°C for 10 minutes, until golden on top, then turn and cook for an additional 10 minutes. Depending on the size that you have cut your chicken, your goujons may need a slightly longer or shorter cooking time. If you want to check for doneness, slice a larger goujon in half to check it is cooked all the way through or use an instant read thermometer to check that the cooked chicken is at least 75°C.
7. Serve the goujons hot, with your choice of dipping sauces alongside. My kids like these served in wraps with salad.

Crispy Chilli Tofu

PREP 10 minutes, plus marinating   **COOK** 10–15 minutes   **SERVES** 2

Tofu takes on flavour wonderfully, so make sure to give this a little time to marinate in the fridge before cooking – it will make all the difference! For the uninitiated, tofu can seem a little scary, but these little nuggets are crisp and moreish and sure to convert even the most determined doubter! This is also a great dish for any vegan guests (just make sure to use vegan mayo!).

1 x 300g block tofu
1 tsp garlic salt
1 tsp chilli powder
1 tbsp sesame oil
60g cornflour
1 bunch spring onions, finely sliced
1 tbsp toasted sesame seeds
1 fresh chilli, finely chopped
1 lime, cut into wedges
cooked noodles, to serve
soy sauce, for drizzling

For the sriracha mayo:

2 tbsp mayonnaise
2 tsp sriracha sauce, or to taste

1. Put your tofu on a chopping board and cut into bite-sized cubes with a sharp knife. Pat the cubes dry with kitchen paper then transfer to a bowl.

2. In a separate bowl, combine the garlic salt, chilli powder and sesame oil, then pour the mixture over the tofu and give everything a gentle stir to ensure the tofu is well coated in the sauce. Cover the tofu and transfer to the fridge to marinate for at least 15 minutes, though you can do this several hours ahead if you want to be organised.

3. Once the tofu is marinated, remove from the fridge and set on the worktop. Lay a flat plate on the worktop next to the tofu and spread the cornflour onto it. Working with one piece of tofu at a time, roll the tofu in the cornflour to coat, then place in the base of your air fryer in a single layer. Repeat until all of the tofu is used up.

4. Air fry the tofu at 200°C for 10–15 minutes, shaking the basket halfway through cooking, until crisp and golden all over.

5. While the tofu is cooking, cook the noodles according to packet instructions and make the sriracha mayo by combining the mayonnaise and sriracha in a bowl until well combined.

6. Serve the tofu on a bed of noodles, scattered with the sliced spring onions, toasted sesame seeds and chopped chilli, and with a wedge of lime alongside for squeezing. Drizzle over a litte soy sauce just before serving and put the sriracha sauce in a bowl and serve alongside for dipping.

Smoky Cod with Shredded Kale & Roasted Red Peppers

PREP 5 minutes   **COOK** 15 minutes   **SERVES** 2

This all-in-one recipe makes a really tasty and vibrant midweek meal and can all be cooked together in well under 20 minutes, making it light on washing up and big on flavour! Depending on the size of your pieces of cod and the air fryer that you're using, the cooking time may vary slightly, so do check that your fish is cooked all the way through and that the flesh is flaking nicely before serving. If you want to be super cautious, use a food thermometer to check that it is up to the correct temperature (see page 32 for guidance).

2 red peppers, stems and seeds removed and cut into bite-sized pieces
2 fillets skinless, boneless cod
1 tsp cayenne pepper
1 tsp smoked paprika
125g shredded kale
olive oil, for spraying
sea salt and freshly ground black pepper

For the dipping sauce:
juice of 1 lemon
200ml Greek yoghurt
sea salt and freshly ground black pepper

1. Lay the chopped peppers directly on the base of the air fryer in an even layer. Cook at 200°C for 5 minutes.
2. While the peppers are cooking, lay your cod fillets on a chopping board and dab with kitchen paper to remove any excess moisture. Sprinkle with the cayenne pepper, smoked paprika and a generous grinding each of salt and pepper.
3. After 5 minutes, push the pepper to the side of the air fryer and lay the seasoned cod fillets in the centre. Spray lightly with oil, then cook at 200°C for 6 minutes.
4. Rinse the kale and pat dry to remove any excess moisture. When the 6 minutes is up, add the kale to the air fryer and cook everything for 3 minutes more, until the kale is crisp and tender and the cod is cooked through.
5. To make the dipping sauce, combine the lemon juice and yoghurt in a small bowl and season with salt and pepper to taste.
6. Divide the cod, peppers and kale between 2 serving plates and serve hot, with the yoghurt sauce alongside for dipping and drizzling.

Mains

Turkish-Style Stuffed Aubergine with Saffron & Yoghurt Dip

PREP 5 minutes   **COOK** 15 minutes   **SERVES** 2

This is a really versatile recipe that is perfect for when you have a glut of vegetables on hand and want something fresh and vibrant. Feel free to swap out the red pepper or courgette for some mushrooms or carrots, or anything else you have to hand! The harissa brings an earthy spice to the dish that I love, but feel free to adjust the amount used to suit the tastes of the people that you're cooking for.

1 aubergine, halved lengthways
1 red onion, roughly chopped
1 red pepper, deseeded and roughly chopped
1 courgette, roughly chopped
1 tsp harissa paste
1 tbsp olive oil
olive oil spray, to cook
2 tbsp pomegranate seeds, to garnish
small bunch of fresh coriander, leaves picked and chopped, to garnish
sea salt and freshly ground black pepper

For the saffron and yoghurt sauce:
pinch of saffron (optional)
120ml low-fat Greek yoghurt

1. Lay your aubergine halves, cut-side up, on a board and use a spoon to scoop out the flesh to make boat shapes. The aim is to make a well just large enough to hold the other vegetables, so don't try and remove all of the aubergine flesh.

2. Roughly chop the scooped-out aubergine flesh, then add to a large bowl along with the chopped red onion, red pepper and courgette.

3. Add the harissa paste and olive oil to the bowl with the vegetables and give everything a good mix to combine, ensuring that all of the vegetables are well coated. Season with salt and pepper and stir again.

4. Spoon the vegetable mixture into the hulled aubergine halves, piling them up nice and high to make a generous portion.

5. Transfer the filled aubergine boats to the air fryer, spray with a little olive oil and cook at 180°C for 15–20 minutes, until all of the vegetables are tender.

6. While the aubergines are cooking, make the saffron dip by soaking the saffron in 2 tablespoons of boiling water for a couple of minutes, if using. Put the yoghurt in a serving bowl, season with salt and pepper and pour over the bloomed saffron mixture. Stir to combine.

7. Transfer the cooked aubergines to serving plates, scatter with pomegranate seeds and fresh coriander, then serve hot, with the saffron and yoghurt sauce alongside.

Chicken & Back-of-the-Fridge-Veg Kebabs

PREP 5 minutes   **COOK** 15–20 minutes   **SERVES** 2
KIT 4 wooden skewers, soaked in water for at least 30 minutes

These kebabs are a great option for when you have a load of veg at the back of the fridge that needs using up. I've suggested tomatoes and peppers in the ingredients lists, but mushrooms, cauliflower or broccoli florets or chunks of courgette or aubergine would work just as well. Chicken thighs are cheaper than breast, but are full of flavour and stay lovely and juicy in the air fryer, so are just not economical but tasty too!

2 skinless, boneless chicken thighs, cut into bite-sized pieces

1 yellow pepper, deseeded and cut into bite-sized pieces

4 cherry tomatoes

olive oil, for spraying (optional)

sea salt and freshly ground black pepper

green salad leaves of your choice, to serve

For the sriracha mayo:

2 tbsp mayonnaise

2 tsp sriracha sauce, or to taste

1. Thread the pieces of chicken, yellow pepper and whole tomatoes onto the skewers, alternating the chicken and vegetables as you do. Season with salt and pepper and spray with a little olive oil, if using.

2. Lay the skewers in the base of the air fryer in a single layer and cook at 180°C for 15–20 minutes, turning halfway, until the vegetables are tender and the chicken is cooked through.

3. While the skewers are cooking, make the sriracha mayo by combining the ingredients in small bowl.

4. Once cooked, divide the skewers between serving plates and serve with your choice of salad and the sriracha mayo alongside.

Mains

Lamb Kofta Kebabs with Yoghurt & Mint Dip

PREP 10 minutes **COOK** 20–25 minutes **SERVES** 2
KIT 4 wooden skewers, soaked in cold water for 30 minutes, food processor (optional)

These flavour-filled kofta make a wonderfully fresh and light meal as they are, but could be served with some chips or wedges alongside if you're looking for something more substantial. If you like a bit of spice, you could add a drizzle of chilli sauce to the filled pittas before serving.

500g minced lamb
1 tsp ground cumin
1 tsp ground turmeric
½ tsp garlic salt
2 tbsp ground coriander
1 egg, beaten
sea salt and freshly ground black
    pepper

For the dip:
¼ cucumber, finely diced
250ml fat-free yoghurt
handful of fresh mint leaves, finely
    chopped
sea salt and freshly ground black
    pepper

To serve:
4 pitta breads
salad of your choice

1. In a large bowl or the bowl of a food processor, add the minced lamb, spices, egg and a generous grinding of salt and pepper. If using a food processor, pulse until everything is well combined. If using your hands, simply mix everything together working until the spices and egg are evenly distributed throughout the meat.

2. Form the spiced meat mixture into 4 even sized balls, then squeeze each ball along the length of one of the skewers to form a sausage shape.

3. Lay the skewers in the base of the air fryer in a single layer and cook for 20–25 minutes at 190°C, turning halfway through, until cooked through.

4. While the kofta are cooking, make the cucumber and mint dip by combining all of the ingredients in a small bowl and stirring to combine. Season to taste and set aside.

5. Lightly toast the pitta breads, then serve the kofta with the bread, salad and dipping sauce alongside.

Loaded Chicken Nachos

PREP 5 minutes   **COOK** 10 minutes   **SERVES** 2
KIT Large silicone mould or heatproof ceramic dish that fits in your air fryer

These nachos are a great way of using up any leftover meat from your Sunday lunch. They are delicious with chicken, but would also work really well with leftover pork or beef – whatever you have handy! If you don't have any leftover meat, then just leave it out or follow the instructions at the bottom of the page to cook a chicken breast from scratch.

175g shredded chicken breast
100g salted tortilla chips
60g Cheddar cheese, grated
handful of fresh coriander, leaves
   picked
1 red chilli, finely sliced
½ avocado, sliced
2 tbsp sour cream

1. Place half of the tortilla chips in the base of your silicone mould or ceramic dish in a single layer. Scatter over half of the chicken, followed by half of the cheese. Repeat the layers with the remaining tortilla chips, chicken and cheese.

2. Place the mould or dish in the air fryer and cook at 160°C for 8–10 minutes, until the tortillas are crisp and the cheese is melted and golden.

3. Garnish with slices of chilli and avocado and dot the sour cream over the dish. Place in the middle of the table for everyone to dig in.

Top Tip

If you don't have any leftover chicken that needs using up, simply spray a chicken breast lightly with oil, season with salt and pepper and cook in the air fryer at 180°C for 15–20 minutes, until cooked through, then follow the recipe as above.

Cheesy Broccoli, Cauliflower & Ham Bake

PREP 5 minutes   **COOK** 15–20 minutes   **SERVES** 2
KIT Heatproof baking dish that fits in your air fryer

This makes a wonderful side dish to serve with a roast dinner, but is also great on its own, perhaps served with some garlic bread on the side. If you want to make it vegetarian, simply omit the ham when assembling the bake.

1 small head broccoli, cut into small florets
1 small head cauliflower, cut into small florets
80g Cheddar cheese, grated
2 slices ham, roughly chopped
1 ball mozzarella, roughly torn
1 tbsp olive oil
sea salt and freshly ground black pepper
fresh parsley, to garnish (optional)

1. Lay the broccoli and cauliflower florets in the base of your baking dish, then sprinkle over the chopped ham. Top with a layer of grated Cheddar and then dot the torn mozzarella over.

2. Transfer to the air fryer and cook at 160°C for 15–20 minutes, until the cheese is melted and golden and the vegetables are tender. Sprinkle with parsley and serve hot.

Pil Pil Prawns

PREP 10 minutes   **COOK** 10 minutes   **SERVES** 2
KIT Heatproof baking dish that fits in your air fryer

These juicy prawns coated in delicious spice make a wonderful meal when paired with hunks of crusty breads for mopping up the juices. Prawns cook quickly in the air fryer, so keen an eye, especially if yours are on the smaller side. This would also make a brilliant dinner-party starter for four and can be cooked quickly, just as your guests are sitting down at the table.

4 tbsp olive oil

200g raw king prawns, defrosted if frozen

2 red chillies (or more if you like it spicy)

4 garlic cloves, sliced

1 tsp paprika

sea salt and freshly ground black pepper

To serve:

a handful of parsley, chopped

crusty bread

1. Pour the oil into your dish, place into your air fryer and heat on 190°C for about 5 minutes – you want the oil to heat up before you add the rest of the ingredients.

2. While the oil is heating, put your prawns in a bowl and add the chopped chillies, garlic and paprika. Stir so they are coated in the flavourings.

3. Carefully add your prawns to the hot dish, giving them a good stir in the oil. Cook for 5 minutes, until the prawns are cooked through. Keep a close eye on them as the cooking time will depend on the size of the prawns and you don't want them to be either over- or under-cooked.

4. Carefully remove your dish from the fryer as it will be super-hot! Serve the prawns with a sprinkle of chopped parsley and crusty bread alongside.

Pasta Sauce

PREP 10 minutes   **COOK** 15 minutes   **MAKES** 4 servings
KIT Heatproof baking dish that fits in your air fryer and a blender,
food processor or smoothie maker

**Yes, you heard it right – you can make your own pasta sauce in the air fryer!
This is yet another great way of using up vegetables you have in the fridge.
It is so versatile and freezes brilliantly too.**

1 red onion, finely sliced
1 red pepper, deseeded and sliced
2 garlic cloves, finely sliced
1 tsp dried oregano
a handful of fresh basil leaves,
    chopped
1 carrot, grated
2 beef tomatoes, sliced
1 tbsp olive oil (optional)
sea salt and freshly ground black
    pepper

1. Start by placing your onion and pepper slices in the bottom of your dish and scatter over your sliced garlic. Sprinkle your oregano and chopped basil over the top. Scatter the grated carrot over and finish by covering the ingredients with your sliced tomatoes. I like to drizzle over some olive oil, but it's not necessary.

2. Set your air fryer to 160°C and cook for 15 minutes. Carefully remove the dish from the fryer and leave to cool a little.

3. Transfer the mixture to a blender and blitz to a smooth sauce. If you like it a little looser, add a dash of water whilst blending. Season to taste with salt and pepper, then separate into containers (if wished) and store in the fridge or freezer until needed. Reheat gently in a saucepan on the hob or in the microwave. Use to dress pasta ot serve with the meatballs on page 107.

Turkey Meatballs

PREP 10 minutes   **COOK** 12 minutes   **SERVES** 2   **KIT** Baking paper

These meatballs are so juicy and tasty and are delicious served with the pasta sauce on page 105. Turkey mince is low in fat too, so these are a great healthy alternative to beef meatballs.

250g minced turkey
1 tsp red pesto
½ tsp paprika
1 tsp garlic granules
1 tsp onion salt
a handful of fresh basil, chopped
1 egg, beaten
120g dried pasta, or more if you like
½ recipe quantity Pasta Sauce (see page 105), or a shop-bought sauce of your choice
freshly ground black pepper

1. Put the minced turkey in a bowl and add the pesto, paprika, garlic granules and onion salt. Season with pepper and add the chopped basil. Add your egg, which will help the mixture bind, and mix the ingredients up with your hands. Scoop tablespoons of the mixture and form them into balls about the size of a walnut.

2. Place the balls on a piece of baking paper in your air fryer and cook at 180°C for around 10–12 minutes, shaking the basket during cooking to ensure they brown evenly.

3. Whilst the meatballs are cooking, cook your pasta in a pan of boiling salted water until tender. Heat up your pasta sauce either in the microwave or on the hob. Serve the meatballs on top of the pasta with the sauce poured over.

Spicy Chicken Wings

PREP 10 minutes   **COOK** 15 minutes   **SERVES** 2 **KIT** Baking paper (optional)

These punchy chicken wings are great for sharing and deliver a real kick! Serve with fresh herbs and lime, as here, or they are delicious with a blue cheese dip too.

1 tbsp garlic salt
1 tbsp paprika
½ tbsp sriracha
1 tbsp vegetable oil (optional)
10 chicken wings
sea salt and freshly ground black
    pepper

To serve:

a handful of coriander leaves,
    chopped
1 fresh chilli, finely sliced
1 lime, cut into wedges

1. In a mixing bowl, combine the garlic salt, paprika, sriracha, oil, if using, and salt and pepper to taste. Add your chicken wings and turn them in the spicy marinade to coat fully.

2. Place the wings either directly into your air fryer or onto baking paper. Set your air fryer to 180°C and cook for 15 minutes until golden outside and cooked through. If you are unsure, use a meat thermometer to make sure the chicken is cooked through – it should read a minimum temperature of 73°F when you insert the probe into the thickest part.

3. Place the chicken wings in a serving dish and serve scattered with the chopped coriander and chilli and with lime wedges for squeezing.

Garlic & Rosemary Lamb Chops

PREP 5 minutes   **COOK** 10 minutes   **SERVES** 2   **KIT** Baking paper

These juicy lamb chops, fragrant with garlic and rosemary, make for an elegant supper but can be on the table in just 15 minutes, making them completely attainable for midweek cooking. I like my chops a little pink but do adjust the cooking times to suit your preferred doneness.

6 sprigs fresh rosemary, leaves picked and finely chopped

6 garlic cloves

30g salted butter, at room temperature

6 lamb chops, French trimmed if possible

olive oil, for spraying

sea salt and freshly ground black pepper

1. Pick the leaves from 3 of the rosemary sprigs and finely chop. Peel all 6 cloves of garlic and crush 3 of them. Set the whole rosemary springs and garlic cloves aside for later.

2. Put the butter, chopped rosemary and crushed garlic cloves in a small bowl and stir until well combined.

3. Lay the lamb chops on a chopping board and pat dry with kitchen paper, then season generously with salt and pepper on both sides. Divide the garlic and rosemary butter between the tops of each of the lamb chops and spread out in an even layer.

4. Line the base of the air fryer with baking paper, then lay the lamb chops, buttered-sides up, on the baking paper in a single layer, making sure that they don't overlap.

5. Spray lightly with oil, then air fry at 200°C for 5 minutes. Open the air fryer and turn the lamb chops, using the whole rosemary sprigs to brush the undersides with a little of the melted butter mixture as you do.

6. Chop the remaining garlic cloves in half and place half a clove on top of each lamb chop, then lay over the whole sprigs of rosemary and cook in the air fryer at the same temperature for another 5 minutes, until cooked to your liking. If you want to check for doneness with an instant read thermometer, the chops should be cooked to 55°C for rare, 63°C for medium and 71°C for well done.

7. Serve the lamb chops hot, with your choice of veg alongside. These would be delicious served with the Perfect Crispy Potatoes (page 146).

Pastry Wraps with Asparagus, Parma Ham & Green Pesto

PREP 20 minutes   **COOK** 10 minutes   **SERVES** 2   **KIT** Baking paper

Crisp golden pastry, moreish salty ham, fresh asparagus and that perennial favourite pesto make these lovely open tarts a firm dinner winner. Serve them with a fresh green salad.

1 sheet pre-rolled puff pastry
plain flour, for dusting
2 tbsp green pesto
2 tbsp grated Parmesan cheese
a bunch of asparagus
4 slices Parma ham
1 egg, beaten

1. Carefully unroll your pastry on a flour-dusted service and cut into four equal squares.

2. Spread a quarter of the pesto onto each square and add a sprinkle of Parmesan cheese. Wrap a few spears of asparagus in a slice of Parma ham, then place them diagonally across a pastry square, so that the tips of the spears are at a corner of the square. Fold a free corner in and over the spear, then fold the opposite corner loosely over that so that you have an open parcel. Repeat to form four parcels, then brush all the exposed pastry with the egg wash.

3. Transfer the parcels to the air fryer, placing them on a piece of baking paper. Cook at 180°C for 10 minutes, or until the pastry is puffed and golden.

Pizza

PREP 5 minutes   **COOK** 8–10 minutes   **SERVES** 2   **KIT** Baking paper (optional)

Yes, it's true – you can do pizzas in the air fryer! You can buy the ready-made bases or make your own; for this recipe I used a ready-made base. You can also experiment with all kinds of toppings too! Just be careful to make sure that your pizza base fits into your air fryer.

1 tbsp red pesto
1 ready-made pizza base
60g grated mozzarella
12 slices chorizo or pepperoni
a handful of rocket, to serve

1. Spread the pesto onto your pizza base and sprinkle over your mozzarella and sliced chorizo or pepperoni.

2. Carefully place the pizza in your air fryer, onto baking paper if preferred, and cook at 180°C for about 8–10 minutes, until the base is cooked and the cheese is melted and golden.

3. Serve the pizza with a handful of fresh rocket on the top.

Sausage & Red Pepper Bake

PREP 15 minutes   **COOK** 35 minutes   **SERVES** 2
KIT Heatproof baking dish that fits in your air fryer

This is a wonderfully warming dish that's perfect for chilly autumn days. I love to serve this with big hunks of crusty bread for mopping up all the lovely tomatoey sauce, but you could also serve it with mash if you prefer. To make a veggie or vegan version, simply substitute the sausages for a plant-based alternative and leave out the Worcestershire sauce.

6 chipolata sausages
1 tbsp vegetable oil
1 large red onion
1 red pepper
1 bulb garlic
1 x 400g tin chopped tomatoes
1 tsp Worcestershire sauce
sea salt and freshly ground black pepper
crusty bread, to serve

1. Start by placing your sausages into your dish and drizzling them with the oil. Cook in the air fryer at 190°C for 10 minutes.

2. While the sausages are cooking, slice your onion and pepper and peel and finely chop your garlic. After 10 minutes give the sausages a shake and add the onion, pepper, garlic and tinned tomatoes. Finish with a good shake of Worcestershire sauce and season to taste with salt and pepper.

3. Return the dish to the air fryer and cook for a further 10–15 minutes, until the sausages are cooked through and you have a nice thick sauce. Carefully remove the dish from the fryer and serve with some crusty bread to soak up the delicious tomato gravy!

Mains

Tandoori Cauliflower Steaks

PREP 5 minutes, plus marinating   **COOK** 15 minutes   **SERVES** 2

Great spice mixes are widely available these days, so you shouldn't have too much trouble finding something flavour-packed to give good old cauliflower a pick me up. Sweet mango chutney and fresh herbs make a great accompaniment.

1 small cauliflower head
olive oil, for spraying
2 tbsp Tandoori rub

To serve:
a handful of fresh coriander
    leaves, chopped
mango chutney, to serve

1. Remove the outside leaves and wash your cauliflower. Slice the cauliflower head into slices about 2cm thick. Place the "steaks" on a tray and spray with some olive oil, then sprinkle over the tandoori spices, making sure to cover both sides. Leave for about 5–10 minutes to marinate.

2. Heat your air fryer to 190°C and place your steaks directly into the basket. Cook for about 15 minutes until golden and cooked through. Serve with a sprinkle of chopped coriander and with mango chutney alongside.

Wild Rice-Stuffed Mushrooms

PREP 15 minutes **COOK** 15 minutes **SERVES** 4

I like to serve these hearty stuffed mushrooms with a garden salad and some crusty bread. The wild rice is packed with flavour.

4 large mushrooms
100g fresh spinach
1 x 250g pouch of cooked wild
   rice
3 garlic cloves, grated
4 tbsp panko breadcrumbs
sea salt and freshly ground black
   pepper

To serve:
garden salad
crusty bread

1. Start by removing the stalks of your mushrooms, so you are left with four mushroom cap bowls. Thinly slice the stalks and set them aside for the filling.

2. Steam the spinach over a pan of just-boiling water for a couple of minutes, then squeeze out as much of the liquid as you can between two pieces of kitchen roll.

3. In a large bowl, mix together the cooked spinach, chopped mushroom stalks, rice and garlic and season with salt and pepper. Spoon the filling into the mushroom caps, then sprinkle the panko breadcumbs over the tops.

4. Place the mushrooms into your air fryer and cook at 180°C for about 15 minutes, checking on them occasionally towards the end of the cooking time, until the mushrooms are tender, the filling is piping hot throughout and the breadcrumbs are golden. Serve with a garden salad and crusty bread.

Mexican-Style Tuna Steaks with Avocado Salsa

PREP 20 minutes   **COOK** 10 minutes   **SERVES** 2   **KIT** Large silicone mould

Alive with the zesty flavours of Mexico these fiery tuna steaks, served on a bed of delicious roasted vegetables are soothed with a creamy avocado salsa. They are delicious served as they are, but you could also serve them loaded them into soft tortilla wraps for an extra-special treat.

2 tuna steaks (you can use frozen, but defrost before cooking)
1 tsp coriander seeds
1 red pepper, finely sliced
1 red onion, finely sliced
1 tsp paprika
½ tsp crushed chilli flakes
finely grated zest of 1 lime
1 tbsp olive oil
sea salt and freshly ground black pepper

For the avocado salsa:

1 avocado
a handful of fresh coriander
3 small tomatoes
juice of 1 lime

1. Remove your tuna steaks from the fridge, dry them on a piece of kitchen roll and set aside. Crush your coriander seeds, either with a pestle and mortar, or with the flat side of a knife.

2. Place your sliced pepper and onion in a bowl and add the crushed coriander seeds, paprika, chilli flakes, grated lime zest and olive oil. Season and give this mixture a good mix.

3. Place your tuna steaks and your vegetable mix in your silicone moulds and place in the air fryer. Cook at 190°C for 8–10 minutes until the vegetables are tender and the tuna is cooked but still a little pink in the middle.

4. While the tuna is cooking, make your avocado salsa. Peel and slice your avocado and add to a mixing bowl. Chop your fresh coriander and add that to your avocado. Wash and dice your tomatoes and add these to your salsa along with the juice of your lime. Season well to taste, then serve alongside the tuna steaks.

Vegan Hot Dogs with Balsamic Onions

PREP 10 minutes   **COOK** 20 minutes   **SERVES** 6   **KIT** 1–2 small silicone moulds

Sweet fried onions are an essential ingredient in a classic hot dog, if you ask me, and adding balsamic to them only makes them sweeter and more irresistible. These are great served with my skinny fries and red onions on page 144.

1 brown onion
1 tbsp balsamic vinegar
1 tsp olive oil
6 vegetarian hot dogs
6 hot dog buns
sea salt and freshly ground black
   pepper
condiments of your choice
   (optional), to serve

1. Slice your onion lengthways and place into a small silicone mould – depending on how big your onion is, you may need two silicone moulds. Pour over the balsamic vinegar, add a little olive oil, season with salt and pepper and set aside.

2. Place your hot dogs into the air fryer and cook at 180°C for 8–10 minutes. When the time is up, turn your sausages over and add your silicone cups of onions to the fryer. Cook for a further 10 minutes, stirring your onions halfway through cooking.

3. Place your hot dogs into the buns and add a spoonful of balsamic onions on the top. Serve as is, or with whatever condiments you like.

Jerk Chicken Drumsticks

PREP 15 minutes, plus marinating   **COOK** 20–25 minutes   **SERVES** 4

This is one of those dishes that is just begging for a sunny day and a cold beer (and ideally a Caribbean beach, but you can't have everything!). The marinade can be made ahead and kept in a jar in the fridge for up to a week if you want to be organised. My top tip here is not to skimp on the marinating time, a few hours is ok, but for maximum flavour you really need to make these a day ahead and leave them overnight to soak up all that flavour. The recipe below is fiery without being volcanic, but feel free to add or lessen the chilli to suit your family's tolerance level.

8 chicken drumsticks

For the jerk sauce:

3 small red chillies, roughly
    chopped
1 small red onion, roughly
    chopped
4 spring onions, roughly chopped
4 garlic cloves
1 tbsp white wine vinegar
2 tbsp soy sauce
thumb-sized piece fresh ginger,
    peeled and roughly chopped
2 tbsp brown sugar
1 tbsp vegetable oil
juice of 1 lime
½ tsp ground allspice
1 tsp runny honey
sea salt and freshly ground black
    pepper

1. Make the jerk sauce by putting all of the ingredients in a blender or smoothie maker and blending to a smooth paste. If the mixture is too thick and doesn't blend, add a little more oil to loosen slightly.

2. Lay the chicken drumsticks in the base of a lidded container, then pour over the sauce and rub into the chicken to ensure everything is well coated. Cover with a lid and transfer to the fridge to marinate, ideally overnight.

3. Once the chicken is marinated, lay it in the base of the air fryer in a single layer (you may need to do this in batches, depending on the size of your fryer) and cook at 180°C for 20–25 minutes, turning the drumsticks halfway through cooking time, until the meat is tender and the juices and run clear.

4. Serve hot. These are wonderful to serve alongside salads and slaws, or with rice and peas for a true taste of the Caribbean sunshine.

Teriyaki Salmon with Broccoli & Green Beans

PREP 15 minutes, plus marinating   **COOK** 25 minutes   **SERVES** 2
KIT Small saucepan (optional) and baking paper or a large silicone liner

Teriyaki is a cupboard staple for me; you can make it yourselves (as in the recipe below), or you can buy a variety of brands, all varying in price. One bottle should last you three to four servings. I like to marinade my salmon overnight if I can, to give the salmon time to soak up all the flavours.

2 salmon fillets
200g green beans, trimmed
½ head broccoli
cooked rice, to serve (optional)

For the teriyaki sauce:

4 tbsp light soy sauce
1 tbsp brown sugar
thumb-sized piece fresh ginger,
    peeled and grated
2 garlic cloves, grated

1. To make the teriyaki sauce, combine all the ingredients in a small saucepan with 1 tablespoon water. Simmer gently for a few minutes, stirring frequently, until the sugar dissolves and you end up with a thick, silky consistency to your sauce. Allow to cool.

2. To prepare the salmon fillets, place them in a dish and pour over the cooled teriyaki sauce. Cover and leave to marinate in the fridge for at least an hour, or preferably overnight.

3. Once marinated, place your salmon fillets onto a piece of baking paper or a silicone liner. Transfer to the air fryer and cook at 190°C for 10 minutes.

4. Whilst the salmon is cooking, prep your veg. Wash the beans and broccoli and cut the broccoli into florets. After the salmon has been cooking for 10 minutes, add the vegetables to the fryer, arranging them around the salmon (these can go directly onto the basket). Cook for a further 5 minutes or so – keep an eye on it as the thickness of the salmon fillets will affect the cooking time and thicker fillets may take a little longer. Serve the salmon with the veg, and perhaps a side of rice.

Steak Fajitas

PREP 15 minutes   **COOK** 15 minutes   **SERVES** 2
KIT Heatproof baking dish that fits in your air fryer

These always go down so well with the family! I put all the elements on the table and let people build their own dinner. This recipe is for two, but you can just double it up to serve a larger bunch.

2 medium-sized rump steaks,
    sliced into strips
1 white onion, finely sliced
1 red pepper, sliced
1 tbsp olive oil
1 tsp cayenne pepper
1 tsp chilli powder, or more to
    taste
1 tsp garlic powder
1 tsp paprika
sea salt and freshly ground black
    pepper

To serve:
small tortilla wraps
sour cream
a handful of fresh coriander,
    chopped
1 fresh red chilli, finely chopped
1 lime, sliced into wedges

1. Put the steak in your ovenproof dish along with the sliced onion and pepper. Add the oil and give the mixture a stir. Sprinkle in the cayenne pepper, chilli powder, garlic powder and paprika and season with salt and pepper. If you like it spicy, you can add more chilli powder. Give the mixture a stir, making sure the spices coat the meat and vegetables.

2. Place the dish in the air fryer and cook at 190°C for 10–15 minutes, giving it a stir during cooking, until everything is cooked and browning. Carefully remove the dish from the fryer.

3. To assemble your fajitas, start by adding a spoonful of sour cream dip to a tortilla wrap, then pile some of the spiced meat and veg on top. Sprinkle over some fresh coriander and chopped chilli and finish with a squeeze of lime. Enjoy!

Side
Dishes

So much more than just chips!

Brussels Sprouts with Grated Parmesan & Fresh Chilli

PREP 5 minutes **COOK** 10 minutes **SERVES** 2–4

This deliciously crispy, cheesy, spicy recipe for Brussels sprouts will have you loving these green beauties. Is there anything you can't air-fry?

300g Brussels sprouts
½ fresh red chilli, finely chopped
10g grated Parmesan cheese
sea salt and freshly ground black
  pepper

1. Wash your Brussel sprouts and remove the outer few leaves. Place them directly into the air fryer and cook at 160°C for 10 minutes, giving them a shake halfway through the cooking time, until tender but still retaining some bite. If the sprouts are on the larger size, you may need to air-fry them for longer.

2. Remove your Brussels from the air fryer, place them in a serving bowl and grate the Parmesan cheese over the top.

3. Finally, sprinkle over finely chopped chilli, give the Brussels a shake and serve.

Crispy Carrot Chips

PREP 5 minutes   **COOK** 10 minutes   **SERVES** 2–4

These crispy carrot chips taste indulgent, but don't be fooled because they are super healthy making them a brilliant addition to any meal, especially if you have chip-mad children to cater for!

4 carrots
1 tsp paprika
½ tsp chilli powder
2 tsp olive oil

For the sriracha mayo:

2 tbsp mayonnaise
1 tsp sriracha sauce, or to taste

1. Peel and slice the carrots lengthways, into chip-like batons.

2. Place them in a bowl, add 2–4 sprays of olive oil and your paprika. Stir to combine, making sure all the carrots are evenly coated in the oil and paprika.

3. Place them in your air fryer at 200°C for 8–10 minutes and cook until golden, shaking halfway through cooking time.

4. While the chips are cooking, make the sriracha mayo by combining the ingredients in small bowl.

5. Serve hot, with the sriracha mayonnaise alongside for dipping. These work brilliantly with any dish that you might serve traditional chips or fries alongside.

Bombay Potatoes

PREP 5 minutes   **COOK** 10 minutes   **SERVES** 2

These deliciously fragrant, spiced potatoes make a wonderfully warming side dish to your favourite curry. They are also an unbeatable snack served alongside Friday-night beers. Feel free to adjust the level of spice to suit your taste – if you're making these for children then you can omit the chilli powder completely.

2 large white potatoes, peeled and cut into bite-sized cubes (400g)

1 tsp garlic salt

1 tsp chilli powder

1 tsp curry powder

1 tsp ground cumin

2 tsp vegetable oil, for spraying (optional)

¼ bunch of coriander, freshly chopped, to garnish (15g)

1 tbsp mango chutney to serve (optional)

1 tbsp raita, to serve (optional)

1. Put your bite-sized potatoes in a large bowl and add the garlic salt, chilli powder, curry powder and ground cumin. Toss the potatoes in the spices until each one is evenly coated. For even crispier potatoes spray with a little oil – 2–3 sprays – and toss again.

2. Transfer the potatoes to your air fryer in a single layer and cook at 200°C for 10 minutes until golden, giving them a shake halfway through cooking time. Return them to the air fryer for another 5 minutes if required.

3. Serve the potatoes with the fresh coriander. Add generous servings of mango chutney and raita alongside.

Loaded Sweet Potato Wedges

PREP 5 minutes   **COOK** 15 minutes   **SERVES** 2 as a main or 4 as a snack or side
KIT Heatproof dish that fits in your air fryer

This is a brilliant Friday-night dinner for those days when you've got a movie racked up and the whole family just wants to dig into something really tasty and super easy. I've used sweet potatoes here, but you could just as easily use 'normal' potatoes if that's what you have to hand.

2 large or 3 medium sweet
    potatoes, peeled and cut into
    wedges
1 tsp chilli powder
1 tsp paprika
1 tsp vegetable oil
75g diced chorizo
200g grated mozzarella cheese
sour cream, for dipping
a few chive sprigs, finely chopped,
    to garnish (optional)

1. Put the sweet potato wedges in a large bowl, then add the chilli powder, paprika and vegetable oil and stir until the wedges are well coated in the spice mixture.

2. Tip the coated wedges into the base of the air fryer and cook for 10 minutes, giving the basket a shake halfway through the cooking time.

3. Once part-cooked, transfer the edges to a heatproof dish that fits in the base of your air fryer. Scatter over the chopped chorizo followed by the grated mozzarella, then transfer the dish to the air fryer and cook at 200°C for 5 minutes, until the cheese is melted and bubbling, the chorizo is crisp and the wedges are tender.

4. Remove the dish from the air fryer (being careful as you do, because it will be very hot!), then dot the top of the dish with sour cream and garnish with a few chopped chives, if using.

5. I like to put this in the middle of the table and let everyone dig in for a fun, informal supper, but transfer to plates if you prefer. Serve hot.

Simply Humble Wedges

PREP 5 minutes **COOK** 15–20 minutes **SERVES** 2–4

I couldn't put together a book of air-fryer recipes without including a recipe for classic potato wedges. They might seem supremely simple, but for most people it's the first thing that they try and cook when they first plug in their machine.
Classics are classic for a reason!

4–6 similar size white potatoes (400g)

1 tsp of Cajun spice

1 tsp garlic powder

1 tbsp olive oil

ketchup or mayonnaise, for dipping

1. I like to remove my potato skins for my wedges, but leave them on if you prefer yours that way.

2. Chop your potatoes into wedges and place them in a large bowl. Spray with a little olive oil and add Cajun spice and garlic powder, making sure the wedges are covered evenly with the spice mix.

3. Place them in your air fryer at 200°C for 15 minutes, giving them a few shakes during the cooking time. Cook for an additional 5 minutes for extra crispy wedges.

4. Serve hot with your favourite sauces alongside for dipping and indulge!

Skinny Fries with Red Onions, Garlic & Rosemary

PREP 5 minutes, plus soaking   **COOK** 18 minutes   **SERVES** 2–4

In 2020 when I was first gifted my air fryer the only thing I knew was that it could save me a huge amount on energy, and that it could cook chips! So, I made it my mission to discover what other meals you could create too. Of course, you can cook frozen chips in the air fryer, and the beauty is you don't need any oil at all. They always come out super crunchy and tasty.

The rule of thumb for me is that skinny fries go in at 200°C for 10 minutes. The chunkier the chip the longer they take to cook, always shake halfway through cooking time and make sure you don't overfill the basket!

2–4 medium potatoes (400g)
1–2 red onions, roughly sliced
4 garlic cloves
2 sprigs of fresh rosemary, leaves roughly chopped
1–2 tsp olive oil

1. I like these made skin-on, but if you prefer a 'clean' fry then peel your potatoes first, then slice lengthways into thin batons. Transfer to a bowl of water and leave to soak or around an hour – this removes the starch from the potato and will help make your fries super crispy.

2. Drain the potatoes and rub them with a clean tea towel to remove as much of the water as possible. Transfer to the air fryer and cook at 200°C for 5 minutes, then open the fryer, add the onions, whole garlic cloves and chopped rosemary and give the pan a shake. Cook for another 8–10 minutes, shaking occasionally, until the fries are crisp. Serve hot.

Top Tip

Remember, the more ingredients that are in the air fryer, the longer they will take to cook, so increase your time by a further 5 minutes if your fryer is very full.

Side Dishes

Perfect Crispy Potatoes

PREP 5 minutes   **COOK** 10 minutes   **SERVES** 2–4

**These delightfully crispy potatoes are somewhere between a chip and a crisp and make
a brilliant accompaniment to almost any dish. I also love to eat these as snack served
with fresh rosemary, sea salt and a delicious sauce to dip them in.**

2–4 medium potatoes (400g),
   peeled
1–2 tsp olive oil
2 sprigs of fresh rosemary,
   leaves roughly chopped, to
   serve
1 tsp sea salt

1. I like these skin-on, but you could peel the potatoes first if you
prefer. Thinly slice each potato horizontally across the middle
to make thin circular discs, like crisps. Transfer to a bowl
of water and leave to soak or around an hour – this removes
the starch from the potato and will help make your potatoes
super crispy.

2. Remove the potato slices from the water and dry with a tea
towel to remove as much liquid as possible. Transfer to a bowl,
spray with a little olive oil and stir to ensure all of the potato
slices are coated in the oil.

3. Place in your air fryer, trying not to overlap the potato slices
too much, and cook at 190°C for 8–10 minutes, shaking the
drawer every few minutes. Depending on how thick you cut
the potatoes, they may cook faster. Serve scattered with the
chopped rosemary and a sprinkling of sea salt.

Top Tip

Shake your potatoes regularly
during cooking, as they will
inevitably overlap. This will
help ensure they get crispy on
all sides.

Friday-Night Garlic Bread

PREP Less than 5 minutes   **COOK** 8 minutes   **SERVES** 2–4

This bread, vibrant with the flavour of punchy garlic, is my ultimate comfort food. It's the perfect addition to make any meal that little bit more extravagant!

4 bake-at-home rolls

For the garlic butter:

4 tbsp salted butter, at room
  temperature
1 bunch of parsley, finely chopped
3 garlic cloves, grated
1 tbsp olive oil
10g Parmesan cheese, grated
1 tsp dried oregano

1. In a small bowl, mix together your butter, parsley, grated garlic and olive oil.

2. Cut five or six horizontal slices across your rolls, making sure not to cut all the way through. Divide the butter mixture between the slices on each roll, then transfer the rolls to the air fryer and cook at 180°C for 8 minutes, until the rolls are crisp and the butter has melted.

3. Scatter the rolls with the grated Parmesan and a sprinkling of dried oregano. Serve hot.

Snacks & Bite-sized

Bite-sized morsels for any time of day!

Samosas with Cucumber Raita

PREP 30 minutes   **COOK** 15 minutes   **MAKES** 12

You can make this dish with or without meat. Either way, it's a great snack to use up your Sunday leftovers! Just add whatever roast meat you happen to have left.

1 sweet potato, peeled and grated

1 small white onion, finely sliced

1 large carrot, grated

¼ cabbage, finely sliced

2 garlic cloves, grated

2 red chillies, finely chopped

2 tsp curry powder

leftover cooked chicken, pork, etc. (optional)

6 large sheets filo pastry

1 tsp black mustard seeds

sea salt and freshly ground black pepper

For the raita:

a handful of mint leaves, chopped

¼ cucumber, diced

4 tbsp Greek yoghurt

1. Grab yourself a mixing bowl and add all the prepared veg along with the garlic, chillies and curry powder. It's at this point you can add your leftover meat – shredded chicken, thinly sliced roast pork etc. Give everything a good stir.

2. Cut a sheet of the filo pastry in half lengthways and place it with a shorter side towards you on a work surface. Spoon about a tablespoon of mixture into the bottom left corner. Flip the corner, including the filling, up so that it makes a triangle shape that sits on over the pastry. Brushing the pastry with water as you go, keep folding the triangle neatly up the length of the pastry – it will seal all the sides of the triangle as you fold. Spray the samosa with some vegetable oil and sprinkle with a few black mustard seeds, then repeat to fill the remaining pastry in the same way to make 12 samosas.

3. Line your air fryer with baking paper – this helps them from sticking to your basket – and place the samosa in. Cook them at 180°C for around 15 minutes, checking on them regularly and turning over during cooking.

4. While the samosas are cooking, make the raita. Add all the ingredients to a small bowl and season to taste.

5. When the samosas are golden and crisp, carefully remove them from the fryer and serve with the raita.

Beetroot & Feta Tarts

PREP 10 minutes   **COOK** 15 minutes   **MAKES** 6   **KIT** 6 silicone cupcake cases

These classy little tarts make the prefect canapes for a party and can be assembled really quickly from just a handful of ingredients, making them the perfect option for fuss-free entertaining. They would also make a wonderful dinner party starter if you scaled them up slightly and served them with a simple side salad.

1 sheet pre-rolled puff pastry
½ cooked and peeled beetroot, grated
100g feta cheese, crumbled
1 egg, beaten
sea salt and freshly ground black pepper
balsamic glaze and fresh salad leaves, to serve (optional)

1. Unroll the puff pastry sheet on its baking-paper backing and stamp out small rounds using a 9 cm/3½ inch round cutter, re-rolling and cutting any scraps of pastry until it is all used up.

2. Press the puff pastry rounds into the silicone cupcake cases so that edges of the pastry come up the sides of the cases.

3. Put a teaspoon of the grated beetroot in the base of each of the pastry-filled cases, then top with a layer of crumbled feta cheese. Repeat the layers twice so that each tart has three layers of beetroot and three layers of feta cheese.

4. Transfer the filled cases to the air fryer and cook at 180°C for 8–10 minutes, until the pastry is crisp and the cheese is golden.

5. Transfer the tarts to a serving platter or individual plates and serve hot, with salad and balsamic glaze alongside, if you like.

Carrot & Beetroot Muffins

PREP 5 minutes   **COOK** 15 minutes   **MAKES** 6   **KIT** 6 silicone cupcake cases

These savoury muffins couldn't be simpler to throw together and make the perfect packed-lunch snack. Feel free to mix up the veg to use whatever else you have languishing in the back of the fridge. To use up the beetroot you could make a double batch, or save it to use in the Beetroot & Feta Tart recipe on page 154.

½ cooked and peeled beetroot, grated
2 carrots, peeled and grated
50g Parmesan cheese, grated (or more if you like it extra cheesy)
1 egg
100g plain flour
1 tsp ground turmeric
1 tsp onion granules
sea salt and freshly ground black pepper

1. Put the grated beetroot and carrot in large mixing bowl and stir to combine. Add the grated Parmesan to the bowl, adding more or less depending on how much cheese you like, then crack in the egg and stir again until everything is well combined.

2. Sift the flour, ground turmeric and onion granules into the bowl and season everything generously with salt and pepper. Stir the mixture until the flour is just incorporated, then spoon the mixture evenly into the silicone cupcake cases.

3. Place the filled cupcake cases in the air fryer and cook at 180°C for 15 minutes, until well risen and an inserted skewer comes out clean, returning the muffins to cook for a couple of minutes longer if necessary.

4. Transfer the muffins to a cooling rack to cool, then store in an airtight container for up to 3 days.

Mini Tortilla Cups with Chorizo & Sun-dried Tomatoes

PREP 10 minutes   **COOK** 10 minutes   **SERVES** 4 as a snack   **KIT** Small circular silicone moulds

These tortilla cups are great to use up any leftovers from your fridge. My favourite combination below just used some of the ingredients we didn't use in the pizzas we made the night before. I love this recipe as you can add whatever you like to suit your taste.

3 tortilla wraps
80g mozzarella, grated
6–7 slices of chorizo, roughly chopped
a handful of sundried tomatoes, roughly chopped
1 small red onion, diced
a handful of fresh basil leaves, roughly chopped

1. Cut out small circles from the tortilla wraps either drawing round a small bowl with a sharp knife or using a cookie cutter. Place each circle into a silicone mould and press them into the base to line the moulds.

2. Fill each cup with cheese, chorizo, tomatoes, red onion, basil and mozzarella cheese, dividing the fillings equally between the cups.

3. Set your air fryer to 180°C and cook the cups for about 10 minutes, until the cheese has melted and the tortilla case has crisped up.

Mini Courgette Pizzas

PREP 10 minutes **COOK** 15 minutes **SERVES** 2 as a snack **KIT** 1 large silicone mould

Skip the stodgy bread and use courgette slices instead for these super healthy pizzas that are a fun bite-size too.

1 large courgette
1 tbsp red pesto
1 small red onion, sliced
80g Cheddar cheese, grated
1 tsp dried oregano
a small handful of basil leaves

1. Wash the courgette and slice it into disks. Place the disks into your large silicon mould.

2. Brush each disk with pesto making sure to cover it. Slice your onion so that you have rings and place two rings on top of each courgette disk. Sprinkle with the cheese and finish with a pinch of oregano over each one.

3. Place your mould into the air fryer and cook for 180°C for 15 minutes until the courgette is tender and the cheese is melted and golden on top

Parmesan Biscuits with Goat's Cheese & Green Pesto

PREP 20 minutes   **COOK** 8–16 minutes   **MAKES** about 24
KIT food processor and 5cm round cookie cutter

These classy little tarts make the prefect canapes for a party and can be assembled really quickly from just a handful of ingredients, making them the perfect option for fuss-free entertaining. They would also make a wonderful dinner party starter if you scaled them up slightly and served them with a simple side salad.

120g plain flour, plus extra for dusting
90g butter, cubed and softened
100g Parmesan cheese, grated
1 tsp paprika
½ pack goat's cheese
a small handful of basil leaves, chopped
1 tbsp pine nuts

1. Put the butter and flour in a food processor and pulse together until the mixture looks like breadcrumbs. Add the Parmesan, paprika and a tablespoon of water and blend again until it starts to clump together into a ball.

2. Tip the dough out onto a floured surface and roll out to about 5mm thick. Using the cookie cutter, stamp out around 24 biscuits. Place them onto a sheet of baking paper, keeping them a good distance apart.

3. Set your air fryer to 180°C, then transfer the biscuits, on the paper, to the fryer and cook for 8 minutes until golden and crisp. Depending on the size of your fryer, you may need to cook them in batches. Once cooked, leave the biscuits to cool on a rack.

4. Once cool, spread a little pesto onto each biscuit and top with a little goat's cheese. Finish with a sprinkle of pine nuts and chopped basil leaves.

Mini Pasta Bites

PREP 10 minutes   **COOK** 5–8 minutes   **SERVES** 2   **KIT** Small silicone cupcake cups

When I make pasta, I always cook far too much! I had some leftover, so I thought as a little snack for lunch I'd make these little beauties! Ham makes a great case for holding all the yummy fillings together and you don't have to use serrano – any left-over ham would be delicious, as well as meat-free slices too.

olive oil spray
cooked pasta
Serrano ham
pasta sauce of your choice
    (I use carbonara)
black pepper
rocket and watercress salad, to
    serve

1. Spray your silicone cups with a little olive oil, then carefully line the cups with the Serrano ham, making sure the base and sides are all covered.

2. Fill the cups with the leftover pasta from last night's dinner, then pour on your sauce of choice. Sprinkle the tops of the cups with a little black pepper.

3. Put the moulds in your air fryer and cook at 180°C for 5–8 minutes until the pasta filling is warmed through and the ham is crisp. Serve with a rocket and watercress salad.

Snacks & Bite-sized

Paprika Chickpeas with Crispy Onions & Chilli

PREP 5 minutes, plus drying   **COOK** 10 minutes   **SERVES** 2–4 as a snack

I don't know about you guys but come 3pm, I'm starving! I just need a quick energy boost to get me through the afternoon and these were the solution – a fab little treat to cook and keep for a few days.

1 x 400g can chickpeas
olive oil spray
1 tbsp paprika
1 heaped tbsp dried crispy onions
1 tsp crushed chilli flakes
sea salt

1. Drain your chickpeas thoroughly in a sieve, then tip them onto a tea towel and leave for about 30 minutes to dry.

2. Tip the chickpeas into a bowl and spray with a little olive oil. Sprinkle over the paprika and stir them to make sure they are all thoroughly coated.

3. Place them directly into your air-fryer basket and cook at 190°C for about 10 minutes, giving them a few shakes during cooking. When they are cooked, remove them from the fryer and allow them to cool a little.

4. Sprinkle over your crispy onions, dried crushed chilli flakes and salt and toss to coat. Once cooled, these will keep in an airtight container for up to a week.

Sweet Treats

Every day deserves a treat!

Banana & Salted Caramel Cupcakes with Biscoff Buttercream

PREP 5 minutes   **COOK** 15–30 minutes   **SERVES** 8   **KIT** 8 silicone cupcake cases

It may seem counter-intuitive to bake cakes in the air fryer but it is perfect for small bakes, such as these deliciously sweet banana and caramel cupcakes. Some air fryers have a special bake function, which reduces the speed of the fan, but these will turn out brilliantly even if your fryer doesn't have this option.

100g salted caramel and milk chocolate

140g unsalted butter, at room temperature

140g self-raising flour

140g caster sugar

1 tsp baking powder

2 large eggs, beaten

2 ripe bananas, sliced

2 tbsp Biscoff spread

For the buttercream:

175g unsalted butter, at room temperature

175g Biscoff spread

350g icing sugar

1. Place a heatproof bowl over a pan of gently boiling water to create a bain-marie. Snap the chocolate into the bowl and stir over the heat until melted.

2. In a separate large mixing bowl, add the butter, self-raising flour, caster sugar, baking powder, eggs, sliced bananas and Biscoff spread and beat with an electric whisk or wooden spoon to combine. Pour in the melted chocolate and stir again until everything has come together.

3. Divide the mixture between the silicone moulds, being careful not to over fill, and carefully place them in the air fryer. Cook at 180°C for 15 minutes, until well-risen and an inserted skewer comes out clean. If you have a smaller air fryer, you may need to cook the cakes in 2 batches of 4.

4. While the cakes are cooking, make the buttercream by beating together the softened butter, Biscoff spread and icing sugar until light and fluffy.

5. Once your cupcakes have cooled, pipe or spoon on your buttercream and enjoy!

Biscoff & Strawberry Tarts

PREP 5 minutes   **COOK** 10 minutes   **SERVES** 4   **KIT** 8–10 silicone cupcake cases

These pretty pastries make perfect quick-and-easy treats to serve to friends and family. They look beautiful, taste delicious and are speedy to make. Put them in lunch boxes, indulge for dessert or enjoy as a decadent afternoon snack with tea!

1 x 270g pack filo pastry sheets
4 tbsp Biscoff spread
200g strawberries, hulled and
    quartered
icing sugar, for dusting

1. Carefully unroll your filo pastry and tear each sheet into 6–8 even squares. You don't need to be too neat with these as they will be layered up in your silicone moulds.

2. Once your pastry is prepared, start to layer the filo sheets into your silicone cupcake cases like nests. I like to layer 3–4 sheets in each case.

3. Add a teaspoon of Biscoff to the base of each filo cup, then transfer to the air fryer and cook at 180°C for 10 minutes, until the pastry is crisp and golden.

4. Once the tart cases are cooked, simply top with the chopped strawberries, dust with a little icing sugar and serve. .

Cornflake Flapjacks

PREP 5 minutes   **COOK** 10–15 minutes   **SERVES** 4–6
KIT Cake tin that fits in your air fryer (square, rectangular or circular are all fine), baking paper

**This is a really simple, fun recipe and a great one to get the kids involved, too!
Don't worry too much about the size of your cake tin - just go with whatever fits best
in your air fryer! These flapjacks make the perfect lunch box snack.**

75g corn flakes
150g salted butter
75g soft brown sugar
30g runny honey
150g porridge oats
50g dried fruits (raisins or
   sultanas work well)

1. Grease your heatproof dish with a little butter then line with baking paper.

2. Melt the butter in a saucepan over a low heat until silky smooth, then add the brown sugar and honey and stir to combine. Remove from the heat and stir through the corn flakes, porridge oats and dried fruits until everything is well combined.

3. Pour your mixture into your prepared tin, then transfer to the air fryer and cook at 170°C for 10–15 minutes, until just firm.

4. Remove from the air fryer and set aside to cool before removing from the tin, slicing into even squares and serving.

Lemon Drizzle Loaf

PREP 5 minutes   **COOK** 10 minutes   **SERVES** 4   **KIT** 450g loaf tin that fits in your air fryer

Everyone's favourite teatime treat made in the air fryer! This zesty cake is such a classic and is sure to have the whole family reaching for a second slice. You will need a larger air fryer to fit the loaf tin inside, but the batter would also work brilliantly for cupcakes if you don't have capacity for a larger cake – simply reduce the cooking time to 15 minutes.

200g unsalted butter, at room
   temperature
200g caster sugar
3 eggs
200g plain flour
1 tbsp baking powder
zest and juice of 1 lemon

For the drizzle:
juice of 1 lemon
80g caster sugar

1. Grease the loaf tin with butter and line with baking paper. Set aside while you prepare the cake batter.

2. In a large mixing bowl with an electric whisk, beat together the butter and caster sugar until light and fluffy. Add the eggs 1 at a time, beating between each addition, then sift in the flour and baking powder and mix again to combine. Add the lemon juice and zest and mix again. .

3. Pour the batter into the prepared loaf tin and level out the top. Transfer to the air fryer and cook at 170°C for 20–25 minutes, checking it regularly after 15 minutes, until golden, risen and an inserted skewer comes out clean. .

4. When the cake is almost cooked, make the drizzle by combining the lemon juice and caster sugar in a bowl. .

5. When the cake is cooked, remove from the air fryer and prick all over the surface with a skewer. Slowly pour over the drizzle mixture, allowing it to cover the surface of the cake and seep into the holes. Leave to cool in the tin, then remove, slice and serve.

Sweet Treats

Irresistible Cookie Bites

PREP 5 minutes   **COOK** 10–12 minutes   **MAKES** 16–20
KIT Large silicone mould or baking paper

Cookies this good couldn't be any easier to achieve! If you fancy you can freeze the uncooked cookie dough in a sealed sandwich bag ready for another day and bake them straight from the freezer – just add an extra 5 minutes to the cooking time. Super speedy and it means you'll have cookies on tap!

150g salted butter, at room temperature
80g light brown muscovado sugar
80g granulated sugar
1 large egg, beaten
225g plain flour
½ tsp bicarbonate of soda
200g plain chocolate chips or chunks

1. In a large mixing bowl, beat together the butter, muscovado sugar, granulated sugar, egg, plain flour and bicarbonate of soda to make a firm dough. Add the chocolate chips or chunks and beat again until well incorporated.

2. Using your hands, break off golf ball-sized pieces of the dough and roll them into balls. Continue until all the dough is used up. (If you don't want to cook all the cookies now, transfer a portion to the freezer to cook at a later date.)

3. You can cook the cookies in a large silicone mould or on a sheet of baking paper. Either way, transfer the cookie balls to the air fryer, spacing them out so that they can spread during cooking and bake at 180°C for 10–12 minutes, until golden but still fairly soft (they will firm up as they cool). Depending on how many cookies you are cooking off and the size of your air fryer, you may need to do this in several batches. Leave to cool slightly, then serve still slightly warm or cooled. Perfect with a cup of tea or a glass of milk and a smile on your face!

Top Tip
If you want to bake larger cookies, just up the cooking time by 5 minutes or so and check the cookies regularly.

Rhubarb, Ginger & Chocolate Chip Cookies

PREP 5 minutes   **COOK** 12–15 minutes   **SERVES** 2–4   **KIT** 12 silicone cupcake cases

Rhubarb and ginger are such a lovely combination – throw in some chocolate and I'm in heaven! These comforting cookies are full of flavour and ready in less than 30 minutes!

200g unsalted butter, at room temperature
100g caster sugar
200g plain flour
1 egg
75g chocolate chips
2 sticks rhubarb, washed and finely chopped
1 thumb-sized piece fresh ginger, peeled and grated

1. In a large mixing bowl, beat together the butter, caster sugar, plain flour and egg to form a dough, then add the chocolate chips, rhubarb and grated ginger and mix again until well incorporated.

2. Place a spoonful of the mixture into each of the silicone cupcake cases – enough to cover the base of each case - then transfer the cases to the air fryer (you may have to do this in batches) and cook at 180°C for 12–15 minutes, until crisp and golden.

3. Remove from the air fryer and set aside to cool slightly, then remove the cookies from their cases. Enjoy warm or cooled to room temperature with a nice cup of tea alongside.

Oat & Banana Cupcakes

PREP 5 minutes   **COOK** 12–15 minutes   **SERVES** 4   **KIT** 8 silicone cupcake cases

Make a day ahead and these cupcakes are the perfect, grab-and-go breakfast for when you're on the move and need a filling, healthy meal in a hurry! These also freeze brilliantly, so you can have a store of them in the freezer ready to go at a moment's notice.

⅔ ripe bananas, chopped into bitesize chunks
1 tbsp maple syrup
3 medium eggs, beaten
2 tbsp milk
1 tsp baking soda
½ tsp cinnamon
40g rolled oats
1 tbsp runny honey

1. In a large mixing bowl, beat the banana, maple syrup, eggs, milk, baking soda, cinnamon, oats and honey together until well combined.

2. Pour the batter into your silicone cupcake cases, being sure not to overfill, then place in the air fryer and cook at 180°C for around 12 minutes, until firm and risen. (You may have to do this in batches.) Leave to cool slightly, then serve. I like to serve these with a dollop of low-fat yoghurt.

Sweet Treats

Index

Index

Index

Thank You

Where do I even begin? I am so fortunate to have some amazing people in my life, but I have to start with a huge thank you to my son, Jack, my best and most honest food critic and source of the most unconditional support that a mum could ever wish for. Don't ever change, I love you.

To my dad, where would I be without you and your endless love and encouragement? You're my biggest fan as I am yours. To my big sis, who is always there for me, just a phone call away – it's not just for wedges, hey! To Nancy and Charlie, words can't even express what gratitude I have for you both. To Will, for being my rock throughout it all. What would I have done without you? Go team! To Rich, for igniting my love for cooking and food, thank you. Emma, thank you for the days out, the walks and the fresh air to help clear my mind – I needed it more than you know. Tracy, thank you for your constant energy and positivity! To my aunty Net, for your continued love and support. And to all my amazing friends and family that I've not mentioned by name, you know who you are, and I love you all.

For the absolutely amazing team at Penguin Michael Joseph, without you none of this would be possible. I will always be forever grateful. The most amazing talents that are Dan Hurst, Aggie Russell, Georgie Hewitt, Danielle Wood, Ted Allen, Katy McClelland, Troy Willis, Sarah Berks, Ellie Morley and Kallie Townsend. You all absolutely rock!

And finally, to the most supportive and amazing Instagram following a girl could ever wish for, you have made my dreams come true!

Meatball Sliders

PREP 10 minutes   **COOK** 10 minutes   **MAKES** 12   **KIT** Baking paper

Using a pack of ready-made meatballs makes these sliders so easy. Just squish them to flatten a little and you have perfect little burgers to fill your sliders. Small slider rolls are not widely available, so I like to use slices of baguette instead, for that lovely combination of fluffy insides and a bit of crunch. For the fillings, I went for tomato, cheese, lettuce, and gherkin, but feel free to experiment and make them your own!

12 meatballs (store-bought or make your own using the recipe on page 107)
2–3 tomatoes, sliced
6 slices Cheddar cheese
12 little gem lettuce leaves
12 cornichons
1 baguette loaf
ketchup, for squeezing

1. Start by laying your meatballs out on greaseproof paper, leaving space between for them to spread. Place another sheet of paper on top, followed by a chopping board and lightly press down to flatten them. Once the meatballs are all squashed, place them either directly into the fryer, or onto baking paper, making sure they don't overlap. Set your air fryer to 180°C and cook for 10 minutes.

2. While the burgers are cooking, you can prep your slider fillings! Thinly slice the tomatoes and cut each cheese slice into quarters. Wash your lettuce and leave to dry on some kitchen roll, then slice the cornichons in half lengthways and leave those to drain on kitchen roll too. Slice the baguette so you have small circular pieces – these will be your buns.

3. When the burgers are ready, carefully remove them and assemble your sliders with a burger, two pieces of the cheese, a cornichon, a tomato slice, a lettuce leaf and a squeeze of ketchup – in whatever order you like.

Snacks & Bite-sized

Broccoli & Cauliflower Bites

PREP 10 minutes   **COOK** 10 minutes   **SERVES** 4–6 as a snack

A simple way to use up any veg you may have left over from your Sunday roast. I had some broccoli and cauliflower florets that didn't make it into my cauliflower cheese bake for our Sunday roast, so, I thought I would reinvent the leftovers as a little snack on Monday. I like to make sure each floret is similar in size, as that way they all cook evenly.

1 small head broccoli, cut into small florets

1 small head cauliflower, cut into small florets

100g plain flour

1 tsp paprika

2 eggs

100g panko breadcrumbs

sea salt and freshly ground black pepper

mango chutney or mint raita, to serve

1. Wash your broccoli and cauliflower florets and pat dry with some kitchen roll.

2. Set up a production line: put your flour in a shallow bowl or on a plate and stir in the paprika; gently beat the eggs in another shallow bowl; and tip the panko breadcrumbs onto a plate. One at a time, dip your florets into the flour to coat fully, then into the beaten egg and finally give them a good covering of breadcrumbs.

3. Put the coated florets into the air fryer and set to 180°C. Cook for 8–10 minutes, depending on size, until golden and crisp. Serve with a mango chutney or a creamy mint raita.

Butternut Squash Sliders

PREP 5 minutes   **COOK** 12–15 minutes   **MAKES** 9–10
KIT 1 large silicone mould (optional)

These are a great snack to turn to when you've got veg in the fridge that needs using up. They taste great and save on waste too! Aside from the squash itself, think of the ingredients listed here as more of a guideline than an actual recipe – I've mixed up this basic recipe with ham, olives and Cheddar cheese, so the world really is your oyster.

top (seedless) half of 1 butternut squash, peeled
80g mozzarella cheese, grated
8–10 slices chorizo (use the salami-style pre-sliced chorizo, rather than smaller slices from a ring)
20 sundried tomatoes
olive oil, for spraying

For the sriracha mayo:
2 tbsp mayonnaise
2 tsp sriracha sauce, or to taste

1. Using a sharp knife, slice the butternut squash into 5mm-thick discs. You should end up with 18–20.

2. Lay half of the discs of squash in the base of a large silicone mould or on a sheet of baking paper set on the base of your air fryer, making sure that none of them are overlapping. Top each disc with a small handful of grated mozzarella cheese, a slice of chorizo and a couple of sundried tomatoes, then top with another slice of butternut squash.

3. Spray the sliders with a little oil, then cook in the air fryer for 12–15 minutes, until the squash is tender and the cheese has melted.

4. While the sliders are cooking, make the sriracha mayonnaise by combining the sriracha and mayonnaise in a small bowl.

5. Serve the sliders hot with the mayonnaise alongside for dipping.